BARRACK-ROOM BALLADS

AND OTHER VERSES

BARRACK-ROOM
BALLADS
AND OTHER VERSES

BY

RUDYARD KIPLING

METHUEN AND CO. LTD.
36 ESSEX STREET W.C. 2
LONDON

First published April 1892
Reprinted seventy-two times
Reprinted 1961

70.4
CATALOGUE NO. 2/3056/1

PRINTED IN GREAT BRITAIN
BY. T. AND A. CONSTABLE LTD.,
HOPETOUN STREET, EDINBURGH
AND BOUND BY
ORROCK & SONS LTD., EDINBURGH

PREFACE

The greater part of the 'Barrack-Room Ballads,' as well as 'Cleared,' 'Evarra,' 'The Explanation,' 'The Conundrum,' 'Tomlinson,' and 'The English Flag' have appeared in the 'National Observer.' Messrs. Macmillan and Co. have kindly given me permission to reproduce four ballads contributed to their Magazine, and I am indebted to the 'St. James's Gazette' for a like courtesy in regard to the ballads of the 'Clampherdown' and 'Bolivar,' and the 'Imperial Rescript.' 'The Rhyme of the Three Captains' was printed first in the 'Athenæum.' I fancy that most of the other verses are new.

RUDYARD KIPLING.

*Beyond the path of the outmost sun through utter darkness
hurled—*
Further than ever comet flared or vagrant star-dust swirled—
*Live such as fought and sailed and ruled and loved and
made our world.*

*They are purged of pride because they died, they know the
worth of their bays,*
*They sit at wine with the Maidens Nine and the Gods of the
Elder Days,*
*It is their will to serve or be still as fitteth our Father's
praise.*

*'Tis theirs to sweep through the ringing deep where Azrael's
outposts are,*
*Or buffet a path through the Pit's red wrath when God goes
out to war,*
*Or hang with the reckless Seraphim on the rein of a red-
maned star.*

*They take their mirth in the joy of the Earth—they dare
not grieve for her pain—*
*They know of toil and the end of toil, they know God's law
is plain,*
*So they whistle the Devil to make them sport who know that
Sin is vain.*

And ofttimes cometh our wise Lord God, master of every trade,
And tells them tales of His daily toil, of Edens newly made;
And they rise to their feet as He passes by, gentlemen un-
    afraid.

To these who are cleansed of base Desire, Sorrow and Lust
    and Shame—
Gods for they knew the hearts of men, men for they stooped
    to Fame,
Borne on the breath that men call Death, my brother's spirit
    came.

He scarce had need to doff his pride or slough the dross of
    Earth—
E'en as he trod that day to God so walked he from his birth,
In simpleness and gentleness and honour and clean mirth.

So cup to lip in fellowship they gave him welcome high
And made him place at the banquet board—the Strong Men
    ranged thereby,
Who had done his work and held his peace and had no fear
    to die.

Beyond the loom of the last lone star, through open darkness
    hurled,
Further than rebel comet dared or hiving star-swarm swirled,
Sits he with those that praise our God for that they served His
    world.

CONTENTS

OTHER VERSES

CONTENTS

INDEX TO FIRST LINES

BARRACK-ROOM BALLADS

▲

To T. A.

I HAVE made for you a song,
 And it may be right or wrong,
But only you can tell me if it's true;
 I have tried for to explain
 Both your pleasure and your pain,
And, Thomas, here's my best respects to you!

 O there'll surely come a day
 When they'll give you all your pay,
And treat you as a Christian ought to do;
 So, until that day comes round,
 Heaven keep you safe and sound,
And, Thomas, here's my best respects to you!
R. K.

DANNY DEEVER

'WHAT are the bugles blowin' for ? ' said Files-on-
    Parade.
' To turn you out, to turn you out,' the Colour-
    Sergeant said.
' What makes you look so white, so white ? ' said
    Files-on-Parade.
' I 'm dreadin' what I 've got to watch,' the Colour-
    Sergeant said.
    For they 're hangin' Danny Deever, you can
        hear the Dead March play,
    The regiment 's in 'ollow square—they 're
        hangin' him to-day ;
    They 've taken of his buttons off an' cut his
        stripes away,
    An' they 're hangin' Danny Deever in the
        mornin'.

3

' What makes the rear-rank breathe so 'ard ? ' said
    Files-on-Parade.
' It 's bitter cold, it 's bitter cold,' the Colour-
    Sergeant said.
' What makes that front-rank man fall down ? ' says
    Files-on-Parade.
' A touch o' sun, a touch o' sun,' the Colour-Sergeant
    said.

> They are hangin' Danny Deever, they are
>   marchin' of 'im round,
> They 'ave 'alted Danny Deever by 'is coffin
>   on the ground ;
> An' 'e 'll swing in 'arf a minute for a sneakin'
>   shootin' hound—
> O they 're hangin' Danny Deever in the
>   mornin' !

' 'Is cot was right-'and cot to mine,' said Files-on-
    Parade.
' 'E 's sleepin' out an' far to-night,' the Colour-
    Sergeant said.
' I 've drunk 'is beer a score o' times,' said Files-on-
    Parade.
' 'E 's drinkin' bitter beer alone,' the Colour-Sergeant
    said.

They are hangin' Danny Deever, you must
    mark 'im to 'is place,
For 'e shot a comrade sleepin'—you must
    look 'im in the face ;
Nine 'undred of 'is county an' the regiment's
    disgrace,
While they 're hangin' Danny Deever in the
    mornin'.

' What 's that so black agin the sun ? said Files-on-
    Parade.
' It 's Danny fightin' 'ard for life,' the Colour-
    Sergeant said.
' What 's that that whimpers over'ead ? ' said Files-
    on-Parade.
' It 's Danny's soul that 's passin' now,' the Colour-
    Sergeant said.
    For they 're done with Danny Deever, you
        can 'ear the quickstep play,
    The regiment 's in column, an' they 're
        marchin' us away ;
    Ho ! the young recruits are shakin', an'
        they 'll want their beer to-day,
    After hangin' Danny Deever in the
        mornin'.

TOMMY

I went into a public-'ouse to get a pint o' beer,
The publican 'e up an' sez, ' We serve no red-coats
    here.'
The girls be'ind the bar they laughed an' giggled
    fit to die,
I outs into the street again an' to myself sez I :
      O it 's Tommy this, an' Tommy that, an'
        ' Tommy, go away ' ;
      But it 's ' Thank you, Mister Atkins,' when
        the band begins to play,
      The band begins to play, my boys, the band
        begins to play,
      O it 's ' Thank you, Mister Atkins,' when the
        band begins to play.

I went into a theatre as sober as could be,
They gave a drunk civilian room, but 'adn't none
    for me ;

They sent me to the gallery or round the music-'alls,
But when it comes to fightin', Lord ! they 'll shove
    me in the stalls !
        For it 's Tommy this, an' Tommy that, an'
            ' Tommy, wait outside ' ;
        But it 's ' Special train for Atkins ' when the
            trooper 's on the tide,
        The troopship 's on the tide, my boys, the
            troopship 's on the tide,
        O it 's ' Special train for Atkins ' when the
            trooper 's on the tide.

Yes, makin' mock o' uniforms that guard you while
    you sleep
Is cheaper than them uniforms, an' they 're starva-
    tion cheap ;
An' hustlin' drunken soldiers when they 're goin'
    large a bit
Is five times better business than paradin' in full kit.
        Then it 's Tommy this, an' Tommy that,
            an' ' Tommy, 'ow 's yer soul ? '
        But it 's ' Thin red line of 'eroes ' when the
            drums begin to roll,

> The drums begin to roll, my boys, the drums
>   begin to roll,
>   O it's 'Thin red line of 'eroes' when the
>   drums begin to roll.

We aren't no thin red 'eroes, nor we aren't no black-
     guards too,
But single men in barricks, most remarkable like
     you ;
An' if sometimes our conduck isn't all your fancy
     paints,
Why, single men in barricks don't grow into plaster
     saints ;
>   While it's Tommy this, an' Tommy that, an'
>   'Tommy, fall be'ind,'
>   But it's 'Please to walk in front, sir,' when
>   there's trouble in the wind,
>   There's trouble in the wind, my boys, there's
>   trouble in the wind,
>   O it's 'Please to walk in front, sir,' when
>   there's trouble in the wind.

You talk o' better food for us, an' schools, an' fires,
     an' all :
We'll wait for extry rations if you treat us rational

Don't mess about the cook-room slops, but prove it
    to our face
The Widow's Uniform is not the soldier-man's dis-
    grace.

      For it 's Tommy this, an' Tommy that, an'
        ' Chuck him out, the brute ! '
      But it 's ' Saviour of 'is country ' when the
        guns begin to shoot ;
      An' it 's Tommy this, an' Tommy that, an'
        anything you please ;
      An' Tommy ain't a bloomin' fool—you bet
        that Tommy sees !

' FUZZY-WUZZY '

(SOUDAN EXPEDITIONARY FORCE)

WE 'VE fought with many men acrost the seas,
   An' some of 'em was brave an' some was not :
The Paythan an' the Zulu an' Burmese ;
   But the Fuzzy was the finest o' the lot.
We never got a ha'porth's change of 'im :
   'E squatted in the scrub an' 'ocked our 'orses,
'E cut our sentries up at Sua*kim*,
   An' 'e played the cat an' banjo with our forces.
      So 'ere 's *to* you, Fuzzy-Wuzzy, at your 'ome
         in the Soudan ;
      You 're a pore benighted 'eathen but a first-
         class fightin' man ;
      We gives you your certificate, an' if you want
         it signed
      We 'll come an' 'ave a romp with you when-
         ever you 're inclined.

We took our chanst among the Kyber 'ills,
  The Boers knocked us silly at a mile,
The Burman give us Irriwaddy chills,
  An' a Zulu *impi* dished us up in style :
But all we ever got from such as they
  Was pop to what the Fuzzy made us swaller ;
We 'eld our bloomin' own, the papers say,
  But man for man the Fuzzy knocked us 'oller.

> Then 'ere 's *to* you, Fuzzy-Wuzzy, an' the
>   missis and the kid ;
> Our orders was to break you, an' of course
>   we went an' did.
> We sloshed you with Martinis, an' it wasn't
>   'ardly fair ;
> But for all the odds agin' you, Fuzzy-Wuz
>   you broke the square.

'E 'asn't got no papers of 'is own,
  'E 'asn't got no medals nor rewards,
So we must certify the skill 'e 's shown
  In usin' of 'is long two-'anded swords :
When 'e 's 'oppin' in an' out among the bush
  With 'is coffin-'eaded shield an' shovel-spear,
An 'appy day with Fuzzy on the rush
  Will last an 'ealthy Tommy for a year.

So 'ere 's *to* you, Fuzzy-Wuzzy, an' your
friends which are no more,
If we 'adn't lost some messmates we would
'elp you to deplore ;
But give an' take 's the gospel, an' we 'll call
the bargain fair,
For if you 'ave lost more than us, you
crumpled up the square !

'E rushes at the smoke when we let drive,
An', before we know, 'e 's 'ackin' at our 'ead ;
'E 's all 'ot sand an' ginger when alive,
An' 'e 's generally shammin' when 'e 's dead.
'E 's a daisy, 'e 's a ducky, 'e 's a lamb !
'E 's a injia-rubber idiot on the spree,
'E 's the on'y thing that doesn't give a damn
For a Regiment o' British Infantree !

So 'ere 's *to* you, Fuzzy-Wuzzy, at your 'ome
in the Soudan ;
You 're a pore benighted 'eathen but a first-
class fightin' man ;
An' 'ere 's *to* you, Fuzzy-Wuzzy, with your
'ayrick 'ead of 'air—
You big black boundin' beggar—for you broke
a British square !

SOLDIER, SOLDIER

' SOLDIER, soldier come from the wars,
' Why don't you march with my true love ?
' We 're fresh from off the ship an' 'e 's maybe give
    the slip,
' An' you 'd best go look for a new love.'

    New love !   True love !
    Best go look for a new love,
    The dead they cannot rise, an' you 'd better
      dry your eyes,
    An' you 'd best go look for a new love.

' Soldier, soldier come from the wars,
' What did you see o' my true love ? '
' I seed 'im serve the Queen in a suit o' rifle-green,
' An' you 'd best go look for a new love.'

13

' Soldier, soldier come from the wars,
' Did ye see no more o' my true love ? '
 I seed 'im runnin' by when the shots begun to fly—
 But you 'd best go look for a new love.'

' Soldier, soldier come from the wars,
' Did aught take 'arm to my true love ? '
' I couldn't see the fight, for the smoke it lay so
     white—
' An' you 'd best go look for a new love.'

' Soldier, soldier come from the wars,
' I 'll up an' tend to my true love ! '
' 'E 's lying on the dead with a bullet through 'is 'ead,
' An' you 'd best go look for a new love.'

' Soldier, soldier come from the wars,
' I 'll down an' die with my true love ! '
' The pit we dug 'll 'ide 'im an' the twenty men
     beside 'im—
' An' you 'd best go look for a new love.

' Soldier, soldier come from the wars,
' Do you bring no sign from my true love ? '

' I bring a lock of 'air that 'e allus used to wear
' An' you 'd best go look for a new love.'

' Soldier, soldier come from the wars,
' O then I know it 's true I 've lost my true love ! '
' An' I tell you truth again—when you 've lost the
      feel o' pain
' You 'd best take me for your true love.

    True love !   New love !
    Best take 'im for a new love,
    The dead they cannot rise, an' you 'd better
        dry your eyes,
    An' you 'd best take 'im for your true love

SCREW-GUNS

Smokin' my pipe on the mountings, sniffin' the
    mornin' cool,
I walks in my old brown gaiters along o' my old
    brown mule,
With seventy gunners be'ind me, an' never a beggar
    forgets
It's only the pick of the Army that handles the
    dear little pets—'Tss ! 'Tss !
      For you all love the screw-guns—the screw-
        guns they all love you !
      So when we call round with a few guns, o'
        course you will know what to do—hoo !
        hoo !
      Jest send in your Chief an' surrender—it's
        worse if you fights or you runs :
      You can go where you please, you can skid
        up the trees, but you don't get away
        from the guns !

They sends us along where the roads are, but mostly
    we goes where they ain't :
We 'd climb up the side of a sign-board an' trust to
    the stick o' the paint :
We 've chivied the Naga an' Looshai, we 've give the
    Afreedeeman fits,
For we fancies ourselves at two thousand, we guns
    that are built in two bits—'Tss ! 'Tss !
      For you all love the screw-guns . . .

If a man doesn't work, why. we drills 'im an' teaches
    'im 'ow to behave ;
If a beggar can't march, why, we kills 'im an' rattles
    'im into 'is grave.
You 've got to stand up to our business an' spring
    without snatchin' or fuss
D' you say that you sweat with the field-guns ? By
    God, you must lather with us—'Tss ! 'Tss !
      For you all love the screw-guns . . .

The eagles is screamin' around us, the river 's a-
    moanin' below,
We 're clear o' the pine an' the oak-scrub, we 're out
    on the rocks an' the snow,

An' the wind is as thin as a whip-lash what carries
    away to the plains
The rattle an' stamp o' the lead-mules—the jinglet
    jink o' the chains—'Tss ! 'Tss !
      For you all love the screw-guns . . .

There 's a wheel on the Horns o' the Mornin', an' a
    wheel on the edge o' the Pit,
An' a drop into nothin' beneath you as straight as
    a beggar can spit :
With the sweat runnin' out o' your shirt-sleeves, an
    the sun off the snow in your face,
An' 'arf o' the men on the drag-ropes to hold the
    old gun in 'er place—'Tss ! 'Tss !
      For you all love the screw-guns . . .

Smokin' my pipe on the mountings, sniffin' the
    mornin' cool,
I climbs in my old brown gaiters along o' my old
    brown mule.
The monkey can say what our road was—the wild-
    goat 'e knows where we passed
Stand easy, you long-eared old darlin's ! Out drag-
    ropes ! With shrapnel ! Hold fast—'Tss ! 'Tss !

For you all love the screw-guns—the screw-
    guns they all love you !

So when we take tea with a few guns, o'
    course you will know what to do—hoo !
    hoo !

Jest send in your Chief an surrender—it 's
    worse if you fights or you runs :

You may hide in the caves, they 'll be only
    your graves, but you can't get away from
    the guns !

CELLS

I 've a head like a concertina : I 've a tongue like a
    button-stick :
I 've a mouth like an old potato, and I 'm more than
    a little sick,
But I 've had my fun o' the Corp'ral's Guard : I 've
    made the cinders fly,
And I 'm here in the Clink for a thundering drink
    and blacking the Corporal's eye.

    With a second-hand overcoat under my head.
    And a beautiful view of the yard,
O it 's pack-drill for me and a fortnight's C.B.
    For ' drunk and resisting the Guard ! '
    Mad drunk and resisting the Guard—
    'Strewth, but I socked it them hard !
So it 's pack-drill for me and a fortnight's C.B
    For ' drunk and resisting the Guard.'

I started o' canteen porter, I finished o' canteen
 beer,
But a dose o' gin that a mate slipped in, it was that
 that brought me here.
'Twas that and an extry double Guard that rubbed
 my nose in the dirt;
But I fell away with the Corp'ral's stock and the
 best of the Corp'ral's shirt.

I left my cap in a public-house, my boots in the
 public road,
And Lord knows where, and I don't care, my belt
 and my tunic goed;
They 'll stop my pay, they 'll cut away the stripes I
 used to wear,
But I left my mark on the Corp'ral's face, and I
 think he 'll keep it there!

My wife she cries on the barrack-gate, my kid in
 the barrack-yard,
It ain't that I mind the Ord'ly room—it 's *that* that
 cuts so hard.

I 'll take my oath before them both that I will sure
    abstain,
But as soon as I 'm in with a mate and gin, I know
    I 'll do it again !

    With a second-hand overcoat under my head,
    And a beautiful view of the yard,
Yes, it 's pack-drill for me and a fortnight's C.B.
    For ' drunk and resisting the Guard ! '
    Mad drunk and resisting the Guard—
    'Strewth, but I socked it them hard !
So it 's pack-drill for me and a fortnight's C.B.
    For ' drunk and resisting the Guard.'

GUNGA DIN

You may talk o' gin and beer
When you 're quartered safe out 'ere,
An' you 're sent to penny-fights an' Aldershot it ;
But when it comes to slaughter
You will do your work on water,
An' you 'll lick the bloomin' boots of 'im that 's got it
Now in Injia's sunny clime,
Where I used to spend my time
A-servin' of 'Er Majesty the Queen.
Of all them blackfaced crew
The finest man I knew
Was our regimental bhisti, Gunga Din.
      He was ' Din ! Din ! Din !
  ' You limpin' lump o' brick-dust, Gunga Din !
     ' Hi ! slippery *hitherao* !
    ' Water, get it !   *Panee lao* ! [1]
  ' You squidgy-nosed old idol, Gunga Din.'

The uniform 'e wore
Was nothin' much before,

[1] Bring water swiftly.

An' rather less than 'arf o' that be'ind,

For a piece o' twisty rag

An' a goatskin watei-bag

Was all the field-equipment 'e could find

When the sweatin' troop-train lay

In a sidin' through the day,

Where the 'eat would make your bloomin' eyebrows
    crawl,

We shouted ' Harry By ! ' [1]

Till our throats were bricky-dry,

Then we wopped 'im 'cause 'e couldn't serve us all

        It was ' Din ! Din ! Din !

  ' You 'eathen, where the mischief 'ave you been ?

    ' You put some *juldee* [2] in it

    ' Or I 'll *marrow* [3] you this minute

  ' If you don't fill up my helmet, Gunga Din.'

'E would dot an' carry one

Till the longest day was done ;

An' 'e didn't seem to know the use o' fear

If we charged or broke or cut,

You could bet your bloomin' nut,

'E 'd be waitin' fifty paces right flank rear.

        [1] Mr. Atkins's equivalent for ' O brother.'
        [2] Be quick.   [3] Hit you.

With 'is mussick [1] on 'is back,
'E would skip with our attack,
An' watch us till the bugles made ' **Retire**,'
An' for all 'is dirty 'ide
'E was white, clear white, inside
When 'e went to tend the wounded under **fire** !
      It was ' Din ! Din ! Din ! '
  With the bullets kickin' dust-spots on the **green**,
     When the cartridges ran out,
      You could hear the front-files **shout**,
  ' Hi ! ammunition-mules an' Gunga Din ! '

I shan t forgit the night
When I dropped be'ind the fight
With a bullet where my belt-plate should 'a' be**en**.
I was chokin' mad with thirst,
An' the man that spied me first
Was our good old grinnin', gruntin' **Gunga Din**.
'E lifted up my 'ead,
An' he plugged me where I **bled**,
An' 'e guv me 'arf-a-pint o' water-**green** :
It was crawlin' and it stunk,
But of all the drinks I 've **drunk**,
I 'm gratefullest to one from Gunga **Din**.
           [1] Water-skin.

It was ' Din ! Din ! Din !
' 'Ere 's a beggar with a bullet through 'is spleen ;
' 'E 's chawin' up the ground,
' An' 'e 's kickin' all around :
' For Gawd's sake git the water, Gunga Din !'

'E carried me away
To where a dooli lay,
An' a bullet come an' drilled the beggar clean.
'E put me safe inside,
An' just before 'e died,
' I 'ope you liked your drink,' sez Gunga Din.
So I 'll meet 'im later on
At the place where 'e is gone—
Where it 's always double drill and no canteen ;
'E 'll be squattin' on the coals
Givin' drink to poor damned souls,
An' I 'll get a swig in hell from Gunga Din !
Yes, Din ! Din ! Din !
You Lazarushian-leather Gunga Din ;
Though I 've belted you and flayed you,
By the livin' Gawd that made you,
You 're a better man than I am, Gunga Din.

OONTS

(NORTHERN INDIA TRANSPORT TRAIN)

Wot makes the soldier's 'eart to penk, wot makes
    'im to perspire ?
It isn't standin' up to charge nor lyin' down to fire ;
But it 's everlastin' waitin' on a everlastin' road
For the commissariat camel an' 'is commissariat load.
    O the oont,[1] O the oont, O the commissariat
      oont !
      With 'is silly neck a-bobbin' like a basket
        full o' snakes ;
    We packs 'im like an idol, an' you ought to
      'ear 'im grunt,
      An' when we gets 'im loaded up 'is blessed
        girth-rope breaks.

Wot makes the rear-guard swear so 'ard when night
    is drorin' in,
An' every native follower is shiverin' for 'is skin ?

---

[1] Camel :—*oo* is pronounced like *u* in 'bull,' but by Mr.
Atkins to rhyme with 'front.'

It ain't the chanst o' being rushed by Paythans from
  the 'ills,
It 's the commissariat camel puttin' on 'is bloomin'
  frills !
    O the oont, O the oont, O the hairy scary
      oont !
      A-trippin' over tent-ropes when we 've got
        the night alarm !
    We socks 'im with a stretcher-pole an' 'eads
      'im off in front,
      An' when we 've saved 'is bloomin' life 'e
        chaws our bloomin' arm.

The 'orse 'e knows above a bit, the bullock 's but a
  fool,
The elephant 's a gentleman, the battery-mule 's a
  mule ;
But the commissariat cam-u-el, when all is said an'
  done,
'E 's a devil an' a ostrich an' a orphan-child in one.
    O the oont, O the oont, O the Gawd-forsaken
      oont !
      The lumpy-'umpy 'ummin'-bird a-singin'
        where 'e lies,

'E 's blocked the whole division from the
rear-guard to the front,
An' when we get him up again—the
beggar goes an' dies !

'E 'll gall an' chafe an' lame an' fight— e smells
most awful vile ;
'E 'll lose 'isself for ever if you let 'im stray a mile ;
'E 's game to graze the 'ole day long an' 'owl the
'ole night through,
An' when 'e comes to greasy ground e splits 'isself
in two.
O the oont, O the oont, O the floppin',
droppin' oont !
When 'is long legs give from under an' 'is
meltin' eye is dim,
The tribes is up be'ind us, and the tribes
is out in front—
It ain't no jam for Tommy, but it 's kites
an' crows for 'im.

So when the cruel march is done, an' when the
roads is blind,
An' when we sees the camp in front an' 'ears the
shots be'ind.

Ho ! then we strips 'is saddle off, and all 'is woes is
    past :
'E thinks on us that used 'im so, and gets revenge
    at last.

  O the oont, O the oont, O the floatin',
   bloatin' oont !
   The late lamented camel in the water-cut
    'e lies ;
  We keeps a mile be'ind 'im an' we keeps a
   mile in front,
   But 'e gets into the drinkin'-casks, and
    then o' course we dies.

LOOT

If you 've ever stole a pheasant-egg be'ind the
   keeper's back,
   If you 've ever snigged the washin' from the line,
If you 've ever crammed a gander in your bloomin'
   'aversack,
   You will understand this little song o' mine.
But the service rules are 'ard, an' from such we
   are debarred,
   For the same with English morals does not suit.
      (*Cornet :* Toot ! toot !)
W'y, they call a man a robber if 'e stuffs 'is marchin'
   clobber
   With the—
(*Chorus*) Loo ! loo ! Lulu ! lulu ! Loo ! loo ! Loot !
         loot ! loot !
            Ow the loot !
            Bloomin' loot !
         That 's the thing to make the boys git up
         an' shoot !

31

It 's the same with dogs an' men,
    If you 'd make 'em come again
      Clap 'em forward with a Loo ! loo ! Lulu !
        Loot !
  (*ff*) Whoopee ! Tear 'im, puppy ! Loo ! loo !
        Lulu ! Loot ! loot ! loot !

If you 've knocked a nigger edgeways when 'e 's
    thrustin' for your life,
  You must leave 'im very careful where 'e fell ;
An' may thank your stars an' gaiters if you didn't
    feel 'is knife
  That you ain't told off to bury 'im as well.
Then the sweatin' Tommies wonder as they spade
    the beggars under
  Why lootin' should be entered as a crime ;
So if my song you 'll 'ear, I will learn you plain an'
    clear
  'Ow to pay yourself for fightin' overtime.
    (*Chorus*) With the loot, . . .

Now remember when you 're 'acking round a gilded
    Burma god
  That 'is eyes is very often precious stones ;

An' if you treat a nigger to a dose o' cleanin'-
    rod
    'E 's like to show you everything 'e owns.
When 'e won't prodooce no more, pour some water
    on the floor
    Where you 'ear it answer 'ollow to the boot
        (*Cornet :* Toot ! toot !)—
When the ground begins to sink, shove your baynick
    down the chink,
    An' you 're sure to touch the—

(*Chorus*)   Loo ! loo ! Lulu ! Loot ! loot ! loot !
        Ow the loot ! . . .

When from 'ouse to 'ouse you 're 'unting, you must
    always work in pairs—
    It 'alves the gain, but safer you will find—
For a single man gets bottled on them twisty-wisty
    stairs,
    An' a woman comes and clobs 'im from be'ind.
When you 've turned 'em inside out, an' it seems
    beyond a doubt
    As if there weren't enough to dust a flute
        (*Cornet :* Toot ! toot !)—

C

Before you sling your 'ook, at the 'ousetops take a look,
  For it 's underneath the tiles they 'ide the loot.
    (*Chorus*)   Ow the loot !   . .

You can mostly square a Sergint an' a Quartermaster
      too,
  If you only take the proper way to go ;
I could never keep my pickin's, but I 've learned
      you all I knew—
  An' don't you never say I told you so.
An' now I 'll bid good-bye, for 1 m gettin' rather dry,
  An' I see another tunin' up to toot
    (*Cornet :* Toot ! toot !)—
So 'ere 's good-luck to those that wears the Widow's
      clo'es,
  An' the Devil send 'em all they want o' loot !
    (*Chorus*)   Yes, the loot,
          Bloomin' loot !
      In the tunic an' the mess-tin an' the boot !
        It 's the same with dogs an' men,
        If you 'd make 'em come again
  (*fff*) Whoop 'em forward with a Loo ! loo ! Lulu !
          Loot ! loot ! loot !
        Heeya ! Sick 'im, puppy ! Loo ! loo ! Lulu !
          Loot ! loot ! loot !

'SNARLEYOW'

This 'appened in a battle to a batt'ry of the corps
Which is first among the women an' amazin' first in
    war ;
An' what the bloomin' battle was I don't remember
    now,
But Two's off-lead 'e answered to the name o' *Snarle-*
    yow.
      Down in the Infantry, nobody cares ;
      Down in the Cavalry, Colonel 'e swears ;
      But down in the lead with the wheel at the
        flog
      Turns the bold Bombardier to a little whipped
        dog !

They was movin' into action, they was needed very
    sore,
To learn a little schoolin' to a native army corps,

They 'aa nipped against an uphill, they was tuckin'
 down the brow,
When a tricky, trundlin' roundshot give the knock
 to *Snarleyow*.

They cut 'im loose an' left 'im—'e was almost tore
 in two—
But he tried to follow after as a well-trained 'orse
 should do ;
'E went an' fouled the limber, an' the Driver's
 Brother squeals :
' Pull up, pull up for *Snarleyow*—'is head 's between
 'is 'eels ! '

The Driver 'umped 'is shoulder, for the wheels was
 goin' round,
An' there ain't no ' Stop, conductor ! ' when a
 batt'ry 's changin' ground ;
Sez 'e : ' I broke the beggar in, an' very sad I feels,
' But I couldn't pull up, not for *you*—your 'ead
 between your 'eels ! '

'E 'adn't 'ardly spoke the word, before a droppin'
 shell
A little right the batt'ry an' between the sections fell;

An' when the smoke 'ad cleared away, before the
    limber wheels,
There lay the Driver's Brother with 'is 'ead between
    'is 'eels.

Then sez the Driver's Brother, an' 'is words was very
    plain,
' For Gawd's own sake get over me, an' put me out
    o' pain.'
They saw 'is wounds was mortial, an' they judged
    that it was best,
So they took an' drove the limber straight across 'is
    back an' chest.

The Driver 'e give nothin' 'cept a little coughin
    grunt,
But 'e swung 'is 'orses 'andsome when it came to
    ' Action Front ! '
An' if one wheel was juicy, you may lay your Mon-
    day head
'Twas juicier for the niggers when the case begun
    to spread.

The moril of this story, it is plainly to be seen :
You 'avn't got no families when servin' of the Queen—

You 'avn't got no brothers, fathers, sisters, wives, or
    sons—
If you want to win your battles take an' work your
    bloomin' guns !
        Down in the Infantry, nobody cares ;
        Down in the Cavalry, Colonel 'e swears ;
        But down in the lead with the wheel at the flog
        Turns the bold Bombardier to a little whipped
            dog !

THE WIDOW AT WINDSOR

'Ave you 'eard o' the Widow at Windsor
 With a hairy gold crown on 'er 'ead ?
She 'as ships on the foam—she 'as millions at 'ome,
 An' she pays us poor beggars in red.
  (Ow, poor beggars in red !)
There 's 'er nick on the cavalry 'orses,
 There 's 'er mark on the medical stores—
An' 'er troopers you 'll find with a fair wind be'ind
 That takes us to various wars.
  (Poor beggars !—barbarious wars !)
   Then 'ere 's to the Widow at Windsor,
    An' 'ere 's to the stores an' the guns,
   The men an' the 'orses what makes up the
    forces
    O' Missis Victorier's sons.
   (Poor beggars ! Victorier's sons !)

Walk wide o' the Widow at Windsor,

   For 'alf o' Creation she owns :

We 'ave bought 'er the same with the sword an
      the flame,

   An' we 've salted it down with our bones.

     (Poor beggars !—it 's blue with our bones !)

Hands off o' the sons o' the Widow,

   Hands off o' the goods in 'er shop,

For the Kings must come down an' the Emperors
   frown

   When the Widow at Windsor says ' Stop ' !

     (Poor beggars !—we 're sent to say ' Stop ' !)

       Then 'ere 's to the Lodge o' the Widow,

        From the Pole to the Tropics it runs—

       To the Lodge that we tile with the rank
         an' the file,

        An' open in form with the guns.

      (Poor beggars !—it 's always they guns !)

We 'ave 'eard o' the Widow at Windsor.

   It 's safest to let 'er alone :

For 'er sentries we stand by the sea an' the land

   Wherever the bugles are blown.

     (Poor beggars !—an' don't we get blown !)

Take 'old o' the Wings o' the Mornin',
   An' flop round the earth till you 're dead ;
But you won't get away from the tune that they play
   To the bloomin' o'd rag over'ead.
      (Poor beggars !—it 's 'ot over'ead !)
         Then 'ere 's to the sons o' the Widow,
           Wherever, 'owever they roam.
         'Ere 's all they desire, an' if they require
           A speedy return to their 'ome.
         (Poor beggars !—they 'll never see 'ome !)

BELTS

THERE was a row in Silver Street that's near to
    Dublin Quay,
Between an Irish regiment an' English cavalree ;
It started at Revelly an' it lasted on till dark :
The first man dropped at Harrison's, the last forninst
    the Park.
      For it was :—' Belts, belts, belts, an' that 's
        one for you ! '
      An' it was ' Belts, belts, belts, an' that 's done
        for you ;
      O buckle an' tongue
      Was the song that we sung
      From Harrison's down to the Park !

There was a row in Silver Street—the regiments
    was out,
They called us ' Delhi Rebels,' an' we answered
    ' Threes about ! '

That drew them like a hornet's nest—we met them
good an' large,

The English at the double an' the Irish at the
charge.

    Then it was :—' Belts . . .

There was a row in Silver Street—an' I was in it
too ;

We passed the time o' day, an' then the belts went
whirraru !

I misremember what occurred, but subsequint the
storm

A *Freeman's Journal Supplemint* was all my uniform.

    O it was :—' Belts . . .

There was a row in Silver Street—they sent the
Polis there,

The English were too drunk to know, the Irish
didn't care ;

But when they grew impertinint we simultaneous
rose,

Till half o' them was Liffey mud an' half was
tatthered clo'es.

    For it was :—' Belts . . .

There was a row in Silver Street—it might ha'
    raged till now,
But some one drew his side-arm clear, an' nobody
    knew how ;
'Twas Hogan took the point an' dropped ; we saw
    the red blood run :
An' so we all was murderers that started out in fun.
        While it was :—' Belts . . .

There was a row in Silver Street—but that put down
    the shine,
Wid each man whisperin' to his next : ' 'Twas never
    work o' mine ! '
We went away like beaten dogs, an' down the street
    we bore him,
The poor dumb corpse that couldn't tell the bhoys
    were sorry for him.
        When it was :—' Belts . . .

There was a row in Silver Street—it isn't over
    yet,
For half of us are under guard wid punishments to
    get ;

'Tis all a merricle to me as in the Clink I lie :

There was a row in Silver Street—begod, I wonder
    why !

    But it was :—' Belts, belts, belts, an' that 's
        one for you ! '

    An' it was ' Belts, belts, belts, an' that 's done
        for you ! '

    O buckle an' tongue

    Was the song that we sung

    From Harrison's down to the Park !

THE YOUNG BRITISH SOLDIER

WHEN the 'arf-made recruity goes out to the East
'E acts like a babe an' 'e drinks like a beast,
An' 'e wonders because 'e is frequent deceased
    Ere 'e 's fit for to serve as a soldier
      Serve, serve, serve as a soldier,
      Serve, serve, serve as a soldier,
      Serve, serve, serve as a soldier,
        So-oldier *of* the Queen !

Now all you recruities what 's drafted to-day.
You shut up your rag-box an' 'ark to my lay.
An' I 'll sing you a soldier as far as I may :
    A soldier what 's fit for a soldier.
      Fit, fit, fit for a soldier . . .

First mind you steer clear o' the grog-sellers' huts,
For they sell you Fixed Bay'nets that rots out your
    guts—
Ay, drink that 'ud eat the live steel from your butts—
    An' it 's bad for the young British Soldier.
      Bad, bad, bad for the soldier . . .

When the cholera comes—as it will past a doubt—
Keep out of the wet and don't go on the shout,
For the sickness gets in as the liquor dies out,
  An' it crumples the young British soldier.
   Crum-, crum-, crumples the soldier . . .

But the worst o' your foes is the sun over'ead :
You *must* wear your 'elmet for all that is said :
If 'e finds you uncovered 'e 'll knock you **down**
  dead,
  An' you 'll die like a fool of a soldier.
   Fool, fool, fool of a soldier . . .

If you 're cast for fatigue by a sergeant unkind,
Don't grouse like a woman nor crack on nor
  blind ;
Be handy and civil, and then you will find
  That it 's beer for the young British soldier
   Beer, beer, beer for the soldier . . .

Now, if you must marry, take care she is old—
A troop-sergeant's widow 's the nicest I 'm told,
For beauty won't help if your rations is cold,
  Nor love ain't enough for a soldier.
   'Nough, 'nough, 'nough for a soldier . . .

If the wife should go wrong with a comrade, be loth
To shoot when you catch 'em—you 'll swing, on my
    oath !—
Make 'im take 'er and keep 'er : that 's Hell for
    them both,
        An' you 're shut o' the curse of a soldier.
            Curse, curse, curse of a soldier . . .

When first under fire an' you 're wishful to duck,
Don't look nor take 'eed at the man that is struck.
Be thankful you 're livin', and trust to your luck
        And march to your front like a soldier.
            Front, front, front like a soldier . . .

When 'arf of your bullets fly wide in the ditch,
Don't call your Martini a cross-eyed old bitch ;
She 's human as you are—you treat her as sich,
        An' she 'll fight for the young British soldier.
            Fight, fight, fight for the soldier . . .

When shakin' their bustles like ladies so fine,
The guns o' the enemy wheel into line,
Shoot low at the limbers an' don't mind the shine,
        For noise never startles the soldier.
            Start-, start-, startles the soldier

If your officer 's dead and the sergeants look white,
Remember it 's ruin to run from a fight :
So take open order, lie down, and sit tight,
    And wait for supports like a soldier.
      Wait, wait, wait like a soldier . . .

When you 're wounded and left on Afghanistan's
    plains,
And the women come out to cut up what remains,
Jest roll to your rifle and blow out your brains
    An' go to your Gawd like a soldier.
      Go, go, go like a soldier,
      Go, go, go like a soldier,
      Go, go, go like a soldier,
        So-oldier *of* the Queen !

D

MANDALAY

By the old Moulmein Pagoda, lookin' eastward to
    the sea,
There 's a Burma girl a-settin', and I know she
    thinks o' me ;
For the wind is in the palm-trees, and the temple-
    bells they say :
' Come you back, you British soldier ; come you back
    to Mandalay ! '
        Come you back to Mandalay,
        Where the old Flotilla lay :
        Can't you 'ear their paddles chunkin' from
        Rangoon to Mandalay ?
        On the road to Mandalay,
        Where the flyin'-fishes play,
        An' the dawn comes up like thunder outer
        China 'crost the Bay !

'Er petticoat was yaller an' 'er little cap was green,
An' 'er name was Supi-yaw-lat—jes' the same as
    Theebaw's Queen,

An' I seed her first a-smokin' of a whackin' white
cheroot,

An' a-wastin' Christian kisses on an 'eathen idol's
foot :

    Bloomin' idol made o' mud—

    Wot they called the Great Gawd Budd—

    Plucky lot she cared for idols when I kissed
        'er where she stud !

    On the road to Mandalay . . .

When the mist was on the rice-fields an' the sun
was droppin' slow,

She 'd git 'er little banjo an' she 'd sing ' *Kulla-
lo-lo !* '

With 'er arm upon my shoulder an' 'er cheek agin
my cheek

We useter watch the steamers an' the *hathis* pilin'
teak.

    Elephints a-pilin' teak

    In the sludgy, squdgy creek,

    Where the silence 'ung that 'eavy you was
        'arf afraid to speak !

    On the road to Mandalay . . .

But that's all shove be'ind me—long ago an' fur
    away,
An' there ain't no 'busses runnin' from the Bank to
    Mandalay ;
An' I'm learnin' 'ere in London what the ten-year
    soldier tells :
' If you've 'eard the East a-callin', you won't never
    'eed naught else.'
      No ! you won't 'eed nothin' else
      But them spicy garlic smells,
        An' the sunshine an' the palm-trees an the
        tinkly temple-bells ;
      On the road to Mandalay . . .

I am sick o' wastin' leather on these gritty pavin'-
    stones,
An' the blasted Henglish drizzle wakes the fever in
    my bones ;
Tho' I walks with fifty 'ousemaids outer Chelsea to
    the Strand,
An' they talks a lot o' lovin', but wot do they
    understand ?
      Beefy face an' grubby 'and—
      Law ! wot do they understand ?

I 've a neater, sweeter maiden in a cleaner,
  greener land !
On the road to Mandalay . . .

Ship me somewheres east of Suez, where the best is
    like the worst,
Where there aren't no Ten Commandments an' a
    man can raise a thirst ;
For the temple-bells are callin', an' it 's there that
    I would be—
By the old Moulmein Pagoda, looking lazy at the
    sea ;
        On the road to Mandalay,
        Where the old Flotilla lay,
        With our sick beneath the awnings when we
          went to Mandalay !
        O the road to Mandalay,
        Where the flyin'-fishes play,
        An' the dawn comes up like thunder outer
          China 'crost the Bay !

TROOPIN'

(OUR ARMY IN THE EAST)

Troopin', troopin', troopin' to the sea :

'Ere 's September come again—the six-year men are
free.

O leave the dead be'ind us, for they cannot come
away

To where the ship 's a-coalin' up that takes us 'ome
to-day.

 We 're goin' 'ome, we 're goin' 'ome,

  Our ship is at the shore,

 An' you must pack your 'aversack,

  For we won't come back no more.

 Ho, don't you grieve for me,

  My lovely Mary-Ann,

 For I 'll marry you yit on a fourp'ny bit

  As a time-expired man.

The Malabar 's in 'arbour with the Jumner at 'er tail,
An' the time-expired 's waitin' of 'is orders for to sail.
Ho! the weary waitin' when on Khyber 'ills we lay,
But the time-expired 's waitin' of 'is orders 'ome
    to-day.

They 'll turn us out at Portsmouth wharf in cold an'
    wet an' rain,
All wearin' Injian cotton kit, but we will not com-
    plain ;
They 'll kill us of pneumonia—for that 's their little
    way—
But damn the chills and fever, men, we 're goin'
    'ome to-day !

Troopin', troopin', winter 's round again !
See the new draf 's pourin' in for the old campaign ;
Ho, you poor recruities, but you 've got to earn your
    pay—
What 's the last from Lunnon, lads ? We 're goin'
    there to-day.

Troopin', troopin', give another cheer—
'Ere 's to English women an' a quart of English beer.

The Colonel an' the regiment an' all who 've got to
    stay,
Gawd's mercy strike 'em gentle—Whoop! we 're
    goin' 'ome to-day.
      We 're goin' 'ome, we 're goin' 'ome,
        Our ship is at the shore,
      An' you must pack your 'aversack,
        For we won't come back no more.
      Ho, don't you grieve for me,
        My lovely Mary-Ann,
      For I 'll marry you yit on a fourp'ny bit
        As a time-expired man.

THE WIDOW'S PARTY

WHERE have you been this while away,
        ' Johnnie, Johnnie ? '
Out with the rest on a picnic lay,
        Johnnie, my Johnnie, aha !
They called us out of the barrack-yard
To Gawd knows where from Gosport Hard,
And you can't refuse when you get the card,
        And the Widow gives the party.
        (*Bugle :* Ta—rara—ra-ra-rara !)

' What did you get to eat and drink,
        ' Johnnie, Johnnie ? '
Standing water as thick as ink,
        Johnnie, my Johnnie, aha !
A bit o' beef that were three year stored,
A bit o' mutton as tough as a board,
And a fowl we killed with a sergeant's sword,
        When the Widow give the party.

' What did you do for knives and forks,
                ' Johnnie, Johnnie ? '
We carries 'em with us wherever we walks,
                Johnnie, my Johnnie, aha !
And some was sliced and some was halved,
And some was crimped and some was carved,
And some was gutted and some was starved,
                When the Widow give the party.

' What ha' you done with half your mess,
                ' Johnnie, Johnnie ? '
They couldn't do more and they wouldn't do less,
                Johnnie, my Johnnie, aha !
They ate their whack and they drank their fill,
And I think the rations has made them ill,
For half my comp'ny 's lying still
                Where the Widow give the party

' How did you get away—away,
                ' Johnnie, Johnnie ? '
On the broad o' my back at the end o' the day,
                Johnnie, my Johnnie, aha !

I comed away like a bleedin' toff,
For I got four niggers to carry me off,
As I lay in the bight of a canvas trough,
      When the Widow give the party

 What was the end of all the show
      ' Johnnie, Johnnie ?
Ask my Colonel, for I don't know,
      Johnnie, my Johnnie, aha !
We broke a King and we built a road—
A court-house stands where the reg'ment goed.
And the river 's clean where the raw blood flowed
      When the Widow give the party.
      (*Bugle :* Ta—rara—ra-ra-rara !'

FORD O' KABUL RIVER

Kabul town 's by Kabul river—
  Blow the bugle, draw the sword—
There I lef' my mate for ever,
  Wet an' drippin' by the ford.
    Ford, ford, ford o' Kabul river,
      Ford o' Kabul river in the dark!
    There 's the river up and brimmin', an'
        there 's 'arf a squadron swimmin'
      'Cross the ford o' Kabul river in the dark

Kabul town 's a blasted place—
  Blow the bugle, draw the sword—
'Strewth I shan't forget 'is face
  Wet an' drippin' by the ford!
    Ford, ford, ford o' Kabul river,
      Ford o' Kabul river in the dark!
    Keep the crossing-stakes beside you, an' they
        will surely guide you
      'Cross the ford o' Kabul river in the dark.

Kabul town is sun and dust—
  Blow the bugle, draw the sword—
I 'd ha' sooner drownded fust
  'Stead of 'im beside the ford.
    Ford, ford, ford o' Kabul river,
      Ford o' Kabul river in the dark !
    You can 'ear the 'orses threshin', you can
      'ear the men a-splashin',
      'Cross the ford o' Kabul river in the dark.

Kabul town was ours to take—
  Blow the bugle, draw the sword—
I 'd ha' left it for 'is sake—
  'Im that left me by the ford.
    Ford, ford, ford o' Kabul river,
      Ford o' Kabul river in the dark !
    It 's none so bloomin' dry there ; ain't you
      never comin' nigh there,
      'Cross the ford o' Kabul river in the dark ?

Kabul town 'll go to hell—
  Blow the bugle, draw the sword—
'Fore I see him 'live an' well—
  'Im the best beside the ford.

Ford, ford, ford o' Kabul river,
    Ford o' Kabul river in the dark !
Gawd 'elp 'em if they blunder, for their
    boots 'll pull 'em under,
    By the ford o' Kabul river in the dark.

Turn your 'orse from Kabul town—
    Blow the bugle, draw the sword—
'Im an' 'arf my troop is down,
    Down an' drownded by the ford.
    Ford, ford, ford o' Kabul river,
        Ford o' Kabul river in the dark !
    There's the river low an' fallin', but it ain't
        no use o' callin'
        Cross the ford o' Kabul river in the dark.

GENTLEMEN-RANKERS

To the legion of the lost ones, to the cohort of
    the damned,
  To my brethren in their sorrow overseas,
Sings a gentleman of England cleanly bred, machinely
    crammed,
  And a trooper of the Empress, if you please.
Yea, a trooper of the forces who has run his own six
    horses,
  And faith he went the pace and went it blind,
And the world was more than kin while he held the
    ready tin,
  But to-day the Sergeant's something less than
    kind.
    We're poor little lambs who've lost our way,
        Baa! Baa! Baa!
    We're little black sheep who've gone astray,
        Baa—aa—aa!
    Gentlemen-rankers out on the spree,
    Damned from here to Eternity,
    God ha' mercy on such as we,
        Baa! Yah! Bah!

Oh, it 's sweet to sweat through stables, sweet to
      empty kitchen slops,
  And it 's sweet to hear the tales the troopers tell,
To dance with blowzy housemaids at the regimental
      hops
  And thrash the cad who says you waltz too well.
Yes, it makes you cock-a-hoop to be ' Rider ' to your
      troop,
  And branded with a blasted worsted spur,
When you envy, O how keenly, one poor Tommy
      being cleanly
  Who blacks your boots and sometimes calls you ' Sir.'

If the home we never write to, and the oaths we
      never keep,
  And all we know most distant and most dear,
Across the snoring barrack-room return to break our
      sleep,
  Can you blame us if we soak ourselves in beer ?
When the drunken comrade mutters and the great
      guard-lantern gutters
  And the horror of our fall is written plain,
Every secret, self-revealing on the aching white-
      washed ceiling,
  Do you wonder that we drug ourselves from pain ?

We have done with Hope and Honour, we are lost
    to Love and Truth,
  We are dropping down the ladder rung by rung,
And the measure of our torment is the measure of
    our youth.
  God help us, for we knew the worst too young!
Our shame is clean repentance for the crime that
    brought the sentence,
  Our pride it is to know no spur of pride,
And the Curse of Reuben holds us till an alien turf
    enfolds us
  And we die, and none can tell Them where we
    died.
    We 're poor little lambs who 've lost our way,
        Baa! Baa! Baa!
    We 're little black sheep who 've gone astray,
        Baa—aa—aa!
    Gentlemen-rankers out on the spree,
    Damned from here to Eternity.
    God ha' mercy on such as we,
        Baa! Yah! Bah!

E

ROUTE MARCHIN'

WE 'RE marchin' on relief over Injia's sunny plains,
A little front o' Christmas-time an' just be'ind the
    Rains ;
Ho ! get away you bullock-man, you 've 'eard the
    bugle blowed,
There 's a regiment a-comin' down the Grand Trunk
    Road ;
       With its best foot first
       And the road a-sliding past,
       An' every bloomin' campin'-ground exactly
          like the last ;
       While the Big Drum says,
       With 'is ' *rowdy-dowdy-dow !* '—
       '*Kiko kissywarsti* don't you *hamsher argy jow ?* '[1]

Oh, there 's them Injian temples to admire when
    you see,
There 's the peacock round the corner an' the
    monkey up the tree,

[1] Why don't you get on ?

An' there's that rummy silver-grass a-wavin' in the
    wind,
An' the old Grand Trunk a-trailin' like a rifle-sling
    be'ind.
      While it's best foot first, . . .

At half-past five 's Revelly, an' our tents they down
    must come,
Like a lot of button-mushrooms when you pick 'em
    up at 'ome.
But it's over in a minute, an' at six the column starts,
While the women and the kiddies sit an' shiver in
    the carts.
      An' it's best foot first, . . .

Oh, then it's open order, an' we lights our pipes an'
    sings,
An' we talks about our rations an' a lot of other things,
An' we thinks o' friends in England, an' we wonders
    what they're at,
An' 'ow they would admire for to hear us sling the
    bat.[1]
      An' it's best foot first, . . .

[1] Language. Thomas's first and firmest conviction is that he is
a profound Orientalist and a fluent speaker of Hindustani. As
a matter of fact, he depends largely on the sign language.

It 's none so bad o' Sunday, when you 're lyin' at
    your ease,
To watch the kites a-wheelin' round them feather-
    'eaded trees,
For although there ain't no women, yet there ain't no
    barrick-yards,
So the orficers goes shootin' an' the men they plays
    at cards.
       Till it 's best foot first, . . .

So 'ark an' 'eed, you rookies, which is always grum-
    blin' sore,
There 's worser things than marchin' from Umballa
    to Cawnpore ;
An' if your 'eels are blistered an' they feels to 'urt
    like 'ell,
You drop some tallow in your socks an' that will
    make 'em well.
       For it 's best foot first, . . .

We 're marchin' on relief over Injia's coral strand,
Eight 'undred fightin' Englishmen, the Colonel, and
    the Band ;

Ho ! get away you bullock-man, you 've 'eard the
    bugle blowed,

There 's a regiment a-comin' down the Grand Trunk
    Road ;

    With its best foot first

    And the road a-sliding past,

    An' every bloomin' campin'-ground exactly
        like the last ;

    While the Big Drum says,

    With 'is ' *rowdy-dowdy-dow !* '—

  ' *Kiko kissywarsti* don't you *hamsher argy jow?* '

SHILLIN' A DAY

My name is O'Kelly, I 've heard the Revelly
From Birr to Bareilly, from Leeds to Lahore,
Hong-Kong and Peshawur,
Lucknow and Etawah,
And fifty-five more all endin' in ' pore.'
Black Death and his quickness, the depth and the
    thickness,
Of sorrow and sickness I 've known on my way.
But I 'm old and I 'm nervis,
I 'm cast from the Service,
And all I deserve is a shillin' a day.

    (*Chorus*) Shillin' a day,
                Bloomin' good pay—
                Lucky to touch it, a shillin' a day!

Oh, it drives me half crazy to think of the days I
Went slap for the Ghazi, my sword at my side,

When we rode Hell-for-leather
Both squadrons together,
That didn't care whether we lived or we died.
But it 's no use despairin', my wife must go charin'
An' me commissairin' the pay-bills to better.
So if me you be'old
In the wet and the cold,
By the Grand Metropold won't you give me a letter ?

(*Full chorus*) Give 'im a letter—
   'Can't do no better,
   Late Troop-Sergeant-Major an'—runs
    with a letter !
   Think what 'e 's been,
   Think what 'e 's seen,
   Think of his pension an'——

  GAWD SAVE THE QUEEN!

OTHER VERSES

THE BALLAD OF EAST AND WEST

Oh, East is East, and West is West, and never the twain
shall meet,
Till Earth and Sky stand presently at God's great
Judgment Seat ;
But there is neither East nor West, Border, nor Breed,
nor Birth,
When two strong men stand face to face, tho' they come
from the ends of the earth !

Kamal is out with twenty men to raise the Border-
side,
And he has lifted the Colonel's mare that is the
Colonel's pride :
He has lifted her out of the stable-door between the
dawn and the day,
And turned the calkins upon her feet, and ridden
her far away.

Then up and spoke the Colonel's son that led a
    troop of the Guides :

' Is there never a man of all my men can say where
    Kamal hides ? '

Then up and spoke Mahommed Khan, the son of
    the Ressaldar :

' If ye know the track of the morning-mist, ye know
    where his pickets are.

' At dusk he harries the Abazai—at dawn he is into
    Bonair,

' But he must go by Fort Bukloh to his own place to
    fare.

' So if ye gallop to Fort Bukloh as fast as a bird can
    fly,

' By the favour of God ye may cut him off ere he
    win to the Tongue of Jagai.

' But if he be past the Tongue of Jagai, right swiftly
    turn ye then,

' For the length and the breadth of that grisly plain
    is sown with Kamal's men.

' There is rock to the left, and rock to the right, and
    low lean thorn between,

' And ye may hear a breech-bolt snick where never
    a man is seen.'

The Colonel's son has taken a horse, and a raw
    rough dun was he,

With the mouth of a bell and the heart of Hell
    and the head of a gallows-tree.

The Colonel's son to the Fort has won, they bid him
    stay to eat—

Who rides at the tail of a Border thief, he sits not
    long at his meat.

He's up and away from Fort Bukloh as fast as he
    can fly,

Till he was aware of his father's mare in the gut of
    the Tongue of Jagai,

Till he was aware of his father's mare with Kamal
    upon her back,

And when he could spy the white of her eye, he
    made the pistol crack.

He has fired once, he has fired twice, but the whist-
    ling ball went wide.

'Ye shoot like a soldier,' Kamal said.   'Show now
    if ye can ride.'

It's up and over the Tongue of Jagai, as blown
    dust-devils go,

The dun he fled like a stag of ten, but the mare like
    a barren doe.

The dun he leaned against the bit and slugged his
    head above,
But the red mare played with the snaffle-bars, as a
    maiden plays with a glove.
There was rock to the left and rock to the right,
    and low lean thorn between,
And thrice he heard a breech-bolt snick tho' never
    a man was seen.

They have ridden the low moon out of the sky, their
    hoofs drum up the dawn,
The dun he went like a wounded bull, but the mare
    like a new-roused fawn.
The dun he fell at a water-course—in a woful heap
    fell he,
And Kamal has turned the red mare back, and
    pulled the rider free.

He has knocked the pistol out of his hand—small
    room was there to strive,
' 'Twas only by favour of mine,' quoth he, ' ye rode
    so long alive :
' There was not a rock for twenty mile, there was
    not a clump of tree,
' But covered a man of my own men with his rifle
    cocked on his knee.

'If I had raised my bridle-hand, as I have held
    it low,
' The little jackals that flee so fast were feasting all
    in a row :
  If I had bowed my head on my breast, as I have
    held it high,
  The kite that whistles above us now were gorged
    till she could not fly.'
Lightly answered the Colonel's son : ' Do good to
    bird and beast,
'But count who come for the broken meats before
    thou makest a feast.
' If there should follow a thousand swords to carry
    my bones away,
' Belike the price of a jackal's meal were more than
    a thief could pay.
'They will feed their horse on the standing crop,
    their men on the garnered grain,
' The thatch of the byres will serve their fires when
    all the cattle are slain.
' But if thou thinkest the price be fair,—thy brethren
    wait to sup,
' The hound is kin to the jackal-spawn,—howl, dog,
    and call them up !

'And if thou thinkest the price be high, in steer
and gear and stack,

' Give me my father's mare again, and I 'll fight my
own way back ! '

Kamal has gripped him by the hand and set him
upon his feet.

' No talk shall be of dogs,' said he, ' when wolf and
grey wolf meet.

` May I eat dirt if thou hast hurt of me in deed or
breath ;

What dam of lances brought thee forth to jest at
the dawn with Death ? '

Lightly answered the Colonel's son : ' I hold by the
blood of my clan :

' Take up the mare for my father's gift—by God,
she has carried a man ! '

The red mare ran to the Colonel's son, and nuzzled
against his breast ;

' We be two strong men,' said Kamal then, ' but she
loveth the younger best.

' So she shall go with a lifter's dower, my turquoise-
studded rein,

' My broidered saddle and saddle-cloth, and silver
stirrups twain.'

The Colonel's son a pistol drew and held it muzzle-
    end,

' Ye have taken the one from a foe,' said he ; ' will
    ye take the mate from a friend ? '

 A gift for a gift,' said Kamal straight ; ' a limb for
    the risk of a limb.

 Thy father has sent his son to me, I 'll send my
    son to him ! '

With that he whistled his only son, that dropped
    from a mountain-crest—

He trod the ling like a buck in spring, and he
    looked like a lance in rest.

' Now here is thy master,' Kamal said, ' who leads a
    troop of the Guides,

' And thou must ride at his left side as shield on
    shoulder rides.

 Till Death or I cut loose the tie at camp and
    board and bed,

' Thy life is his—thy fate it is to guard him with
    thy head.

' So, thou must eat the White Queen's meat, and all
    her foes are thine,

And thou must harry thy father's hold for the
    peace of the Border-line,

' And thou must make a trooper tough and hack thy
    way to power—
' Belike they will raise thee to Ressaldar when I am
    hanged in Peshawur.'

They have looked each other between the eyes, and
    there they found no fault,
They have taken the Oath of the Brother-in-Blood
    on leavened bread and salt :
They have taken the Oath of the Brother-in-Blood
    on fire and fresh-cut sod,
On the hilt and the haft of the Khyber knife, and
    the Wondrous Names of God.
The Colonel's son he rides the mare and Kamal's
    boy the dun,
And two have come back to Fort Bukloh where
    there went forth but one.
And when they drew to the Quarter-Guard, full
    twenty swords flew clear—
There was not a man but carried his feud with the
    blood of the mountaineer.
' Ha' done ! ha' done ! ' said the Colonel's son.
    ' Put up the steel at your sides !

'Last night ye had struck at a Border thief—to-
    night 'tis a man of the Guides ! '

Oh, East is East, and West is West, and never the twain
    shall meet,
Till Earth and Sky stand presently at God's great
    Judgment Seat ;
But there is neither East nor West, Border, nor Breed,
    nor Birth,
When two strong men stand face to face, tho' they come
    from the ends of the earth !

THE LAST SUTTEE

Not many years ago a King died in one of the Rajpoot
States.   His wives, disregarding the orders of the English
against Suttee, would have broken out of the palace had not
the gates been barred.   But one of them, disguised as the
King's favourite dancing-girl, passed through the line of
guards and reached the pyre.   There, her courage failing,
she prayed her cousin, a baron of the court, to kill her.
This he did, not knowing who she was.

UDAI CHAND lay sick to death
    In his hold by Gungra hill.
All night we heard the death-gongs ring
For the soul of the dying Rajpoot King,
All night beat up from the women's wing
    A cry that we could not still.

All night the barons came and went,
    The lords of the outer guard :
All night the cressets glimmered pale
On Ulwar sabre and Tonk jezail,
Mewar headstall and Marwar mail,
    That clinked in the palace yard.

In the Golden room on the palace roof
    All night he fought for air :
And there was sobbing behind the screen
Rustle and whisper of women unseen,
And the hungry eyes of the Boondi Queen
    On the death she might not share.

He passed at dawn—the death-fire leaped
    From ridge to river-head,
From the Malwa plains to the Abu scars :
And wail upon wail went up to the stars
Behind the grim zenana-bars,
    When they knew that the King was dead

The dumb priest knelt to tie his mouth
    And robe him for the pyre.
The Boondi Queen beneath us cried :
' See, now, that we die as our mothers died
' In the bridal-bed by our master's side !
    ' Out, women !—to the fire ! '

We drove the great gates home apace :
    White hands were on the sill :

But ere the rush of the unseen feet
Had reached the turn to the open street,
The bars shot down, the guard-drum beat—
     We held the dovecot still.

A face looked down in the gathering day,
     And laughing spoke from the wall :
' Ohé, they mourn here : let me by—
' Azizun, the Lucknow nautch-girl, I !
' When the house is rotten, the rats must fly,
     ' And I seek another thrall.

' For I ruled the King as ne'er did Queen,—
     ' To-night the Queens rule me !
' Guard them safely, but let me go,
' Or ever they pay the debt they owe
' In scourge and torture ! '   She leaped below,
     And the grim guard watched her flee.

They knew that the King had spent his soul
     On a North-bred dancing-girl :
That he prayed to a flat-nosed Lucknow god,
And kissed the ground where her feet had trod,
And doomed to death at her drunken nod,
     And swore by her lightest curl.

We bore the King to his fathers' place,
 Where the tombs of the Sun-born stand :
Where the grey apes swing, and the peacocks preen
On fretted pillar and jewelled screen,
And the wild boar couch in the house of the
  Queen
  On the drift of the desert sand.

The herald read his titles forth,
 We set the logs aglow :
 Friend of the English, free from fear
 Baron of Luni to Jeysulmeer,
 Lord of the Desert of Bikaneer
  ' King of the Jungle,—go ! '

All night the red flame stabbed the sky
 With wavering wind-tossed spears :
And out of a shattered temple crept
A woman who veiled her head and wept,
And called on the King—but the great King
  slept,
  And turned not for her tears.

One watched, a bow-shot from the blaze,
 The silent streets between,

Who had stood by the King in sport and fray
To blade in ambush or boar at bay,
And he was a baron old and grey,
 And kin to the Boondi Queen.

Small thought had he to mark the strife—
 Cold fear with hot desire—
When thrice she leaped from the leaping flame
And thrice she beat her breast for shame,
And thrice like a wounded dove she came
 And moaned about the fire.

He said : ' O shameless, put aside
 ' The veil upon thy brow !
' Who held the King and all his land
' To the wanton will of a harlot's hand !
' Will the white ash rise from the blistered brand
 ' Stoop down, and call him now ! '

Then she : ' By the faith of my tarnished soul
 ' All things I did not well,
[had hoped to clear ere the fire died.
' And to lay me down by my master's side
' To rule in Heaven his only bride,
 ' While the others howl in Hell.

But I have felt the fire's breath.
    ' And hard it is to die !
' Yet if I may pray a Rajpoot lord
' To sully the steel of a Thakur's sword
' With base-born blood of a trade abhorred
    And the Thakur answered, ' Ay.'

He drew and struck : the straight blade drank
    The life beneath the breast.
' I had looked for the Queen to face the flame.
' But the harlot dies for the Rajpoot dame—
' Sister of mine, pass, free from shame,
    ' Pass with thy King to rest ! '

The black log crashed above the white ·
    The little flames and lean,
Red as slaughter and blue as steel,
That whistled and fluttered from head to heel,
Leaped up anew, for they found their meal
    On the heart of—the Boondi Queen !

THE BALLAD OF THE KING'S MERCY

Abdhur Rahman, the Durani Chief, of him is the
story told.
His mercy fills the Khyber hills—his grace is
manifold ;
He has taken toll of the North and the South—his
glory reacheth far,
And they tell the tale of his charity from Balkh to
Kandahar.

Before the old Peshawur Gate, where Kurd and
Kaffir meet,
The Governor of Kabul dealt the Justice of the
Street,
And that was strait as running noose and swift as
plunging knife,
Tho' he who held the longer purse might hold the
longer life.

There was a hound of Hindustan had struck a
    Euzufzai,

Wherefore they spat upon his face and led him out
    to die.

It chanced the King went forth that hour when
    throat was bared to knife ;

The Kaffir grovelled under-hoof and clamoured for
    his life.

Then said the King : ' Have hope, O friend ! Yea,
    Death disgraced is hard ;

' Much honour shall be thine'; and called the Captain
    of the Guard,

Yar Khan, a bastard of the Blood, so city-babble
    saith,

And he was honoured of the King—the which is
    salt to Death ;

And he was son of Daoud Shah, the Reiver of the
    Plains,

And blood of old Durani Lords ran fire in his veins ;

And 'twas to tame an Afghan pride nor Hell nor
    Heaven could bind,

The King would make him butcher to a yelping cur
    of Hind.

' Strike ! ' said the King.   ' King's blood art thou—
    his death shall be his pride ! '
Then louder, that the crowd might catch :   ' Fear
    not—his arms are tied ! '
Yar Khan drew clear the Khyber knife, and struck,
    and sheathed again.
' O man, thy will is done,' quoth he ;   ' A King this
    dog hath slain.'

*Abdhur Rahman, the Durani Chief, to the North
    and the South is sold.*
*The North and the South shall open their mouth to
    a Ghilzai flag unrolled,*
*When the big guns speak to the Khyber peak, and
    his dog-Heratis fly :*
*Ye have heard the song—How long ?   How long ?
    Wolves of the Abazai !*

That night before the watch was set, when all the
    streets were clear,
The Governor of Kabul spoke : ' My King, hast thou
    no fear ?
' Thou knowest—thou hast heard, —his speech died
    at his master's face.

And grimly said the Afghan King : ' I rule the
    Afghan race.
' My path is mine—see thou to thine—to-night upon
    thy bed
' Think who there be in Kabul now that clamour for
    thy head.'

That night when all the gates were shut to City and
    to Throne,
Within a little garden-house the King lay down
    alone.
Before the sinking of the moon, which is the Night
    of Night,
Yar Khan came softly to the King to make his
    honour white.
The children of the town had mocked beneath his
    horse's hoofs,
The harlots of the town had hailed him ' butcher ! '
    from their roofs.
But as he groped against the wall, two hands upon
    him fell,
The King behind his shoulder spake : ' Dead man,
    thou dost not well !

' 'Tis ill to jest with Kings by day and seek a boon
by night ;

' And that thou bearest in thy hand is all too sharp
to write.

' But three days hence, if God be good, and if thy
strength remain,

' Thou shalt demand one boon of me and bless me
in thy pain.

' For I am merciful to all, and most of all to thee.

' My butcher of the shambles, rest—no knife hast
thou for me ! '

*Abdhur Rahman, the Durani Chief, holds hard by
the South and the North ;*

*But the Ghilzai knows, ere the melting snows, when
the swollen banks break forth,*

*When the red-coats crawl to the sungar wall, and
his Usbeg lances fail :*

*Ye have heard the song—How long ?   How long ?
Wolves of the Zukka Kheyl !*

They stoned him in the rubbish-field when dawn
was in the sky,

According to the written word, ' See that he do not
die.'

They stoned him till the stones were piled above
    him on the plain,
And those the labouring limbs displaced they
    tumbled back again.

One watched beside the dreary mound that veiled
    the battered thing,
And him the King with laughter called the Herald
    of the King.

It was upon the second night, the night of Ramazan
The watcher leaning earthward heard the message
    of Yar Khan.
From shattered breast through shrivelled lips broke
    forth the rattling breath,
' Creature of God, deliver me from agony of Death.

They sought the King among his girls, and risked
    their lives thereby :
' Protector of the Pitiful, give orders that he die !

' Bid him endure until the day,' a lagging answer
    came ;
' The night is short, and he can pray and learn to
    bless my name.'

Before the dawn three times he spoke, and on the
    day once more :
' Creature of God, deliver me, and bless the King
    therefor ! '

They shot him at the morning prayer, to ease him
    of his pain,
And when he heard the matchlocks clink, he blessed
    the King again.

Which thing the singers made a song for all the
    world to sing,
So that the Outer Seas may know the mercy of the
    King.

Abdhur Rahman, the Durani Chief, of him is the
    story told,
He has opened his mouth to the North and the
    South, they have stuffed his mouth with gold.
Ye know the truth of his tender ruth—and sweet his
    favours are :
Ye have heard the song—How long ? How long ?
    from Balkh to Kandahar.

THE BALLAD OF THE KING'S JEST

When spring-time flushes the desert grass,
Our kafilas wind through the Khyber Pass.
Lean are the camels but fat the frails,
Light are the purses but heavy the bales,
As the snowbound trade of the North comes down
To the market-square of Peshawur town

In a turquoise twilight, crisp and chill,
A kafila camped at the foot of the hill.
Then blue smoke-haze of the cooking rose,
And tent-peg answered to hammer-nose ;
And the picketed ponies, shag and wild,
Strained at their ropes as the feed was piled ;
And the bubbling camels beside the load
Sprawled for a furlong adown the road ;
And the Persian pussy-cats, brought for sale,
Spat at the dogs from the camel-bale ;

G

And the tribesmen bellowed to hasten the food ;
And the camp-fires twinkled by Fort Jumrood ;
And there fled on the wings of the gathering dusk
A savour of camels and carpets and musk,
A murmur of voices, a reek of smoke,
To tell us the trade of the Khyber woke

The lid of the flesh-pot chattered high,
The knives were whetted and—then came
To Mahbub Ali the muleteer,
Patching his bridles and counting his gear
Crammed with the gossip of half a year
But Mahbub Ali the kindly said,
' Better is speech when the belly is fed.'
So we plunged the hand to the mid-wrist deep
In a cinnamon stew of the fat-tailed sheep,
And he who never hath tasted the food,
By Allah ! he knoweth not bad from good.

We cleansed our beards of the mutton-grease,
We lay on the mats and were filled with peace,
And the talk slid north, and the talk slid south,
With the sliding puffs from the hookah-mouth.

Four things greater than all things are,—
Women and Horses and Power and War.
We spake of them all, but the last the most,
For I sought a word of a Russian post,
Of a shifty promise, an unsheathed sword
And a grey-coat guard on the Helmund ford.
Then Mahbub Ali lowered his eyes
In the fashion of one who is weaving lies.
Quoth he : ' Of the Russians who can say ?
' When the night is gathering all is grey.
' But we look that the gloom of the night shall die
   In the morning flush of a blood-red sky.
' Friend of my heart, is it meet or wise
' To warn a King of his enemies ?
' We know what Heaven or Hell may bring,
' But no man knoweth the mind of the King.
' That unsought counsel is cursed of God
' Attesteth the story of Wali Dad.

' His sire was leaky of tongue and pen,
' His dam was a clucking Khuttuck hen ;
' And the colt bred close to the vice of each,
' For he carried the curse of an unstanched speech.

' Therewith madness—so that he sought
' The favour of kings at the Kabul court ;
' And travelled, in hope of honour, far
' To the line where the grey-coat squadrons are.
' There have I journeyed too—but I
' Saw naught, said naught, and—did not die !
' He hearked to rumour, and snatched at a breath
' Of " this one knoweth " and " that one saith,"—
' Legends that ran from mouth to mouth
' Of a grey-coat coming, and sack of the South.
' These have I also heard—they pass
' With each new spring and the winter grass

' Hot-foot southward, forgotten of God,
' Back to the city ran Wali Dad,
' Even to Kabul—in full durbar
' The King held talk with his Chief in War
' Into the press of the crowd he broke,
' And what he had heard of the coming spoke

' Then Gholam Hyder, the Red Chief, smiled,
' As a mother might on a babbling child ;
' But those who would laugh restrained their breath
' When the face of the King showed dark as death.

' Evil it is in full durbar
' To cry to a ruler of gathering war !
  Slowly he led to a peach-tree small,
' That grew by a cleft of the city wall.
' And he said to the boy : " They shall praise thy zeal
' " So long as the red spurt follows the steel.
' " And the Russ is upon us even now ?
' " Great is thy prudence—await them, thou.
' " Watch from the tree.   Thou art young and strong,
' " Surely thy vigil is not for long.
' " The Russ is upon us, thy clamour ran ?
' " Surely an hour shall bring their van.
' " Wait and watch.   When the host is near,
' " Shout aloud that my men may hear."

' Friend of my heart, is it meet or wise
' To warn a King of his enemies ?
' A guard was set that he might not flee —
' A score of bayonets ringed the tree.
' The peach-bloom fell in showers of snow,
' When he shook at his death as he looked below.
' By the power of God, who alone is great,
' Till the seventh day he fought with his fate.

' Then madness took him, and men declare
' He mowed in the branches as ape and bear,
' And last as a sloth, ere his body failed,
' And he hung as a bat in the forks, and wailed,
' And sleep the cord of his hands untied,
' And he fell, and was caught on the points and died

' Heart of my heart, is it meet or wise
' To warn a King of his enemies ?
' We know what Heaven or Hell may bring,
' But no man knoweth the mind of the King.
' Of the grey-coat coming who can say ?
' When the night is gathering all is grey.
' Two things greater than all things are,
' The first is Love, and the second War.
' And since we know not how War may prove
' Heart of my heart, let us talk of Love ! '

WITH SCINDIA TO DELHI

*More than a hundred years ago, in a great battle fought
near Delhi, an Indian Prince rode fifty miles after the day
was lost with a beggar-girl, who had loved him and followed
him in all his camps, on his saddle-bow. He lost the girl
when almost within sight of safety. A Maratta trooper
tells the story:—*

The wreath of banquet overnight lay withered on
    the neck,
  Our hands and scarves were saffron-dyed for signal
    of despair,
When we went forth to Paniput to battle with the
    Mlech,—
  Ere we came back from Paniput and left a king-
    dom there.

Thrice thirty thousand men were we to force the
    Jumna fords—
  The hawk-winged horse of Damajee, mailed
    squadrons of the Bhao,

Stark levies of the southern hills, the Deccan's
    sharpest swords,
  And he the harlot's traitor son the goatherd
    Mulhar Rao !

Thrice thirty thousand men were we before the mists
    had cleared,
  The low white mists of morning heard the war-
    conch scream and bray ;
We called upon Bhowani and we gripped them by
    the beard,
  We rolled upon them like a flood and washed their
    ranks away.

The children of the hills of Khost before our lances
    ran,
  We drove the black Rohillas back as cattle to the
    pen ;
Twas then we needed Mulhar Rao to end what we
    began,
  A thousand men had saved the charge ; he fled
    the field with ten !

There was no room to clear a sword—no power to
strike a blow,
For foot to foot, ay, breast to breast, the battle
held us fast—
Save where the naked hill-men ran, and stabbing
from below
Brought down the horse and rider and we trampled
them and passed.

To left the roar of musketry rang like a falling
flood—
To right the sunshine rippled red from redder
lance and blade—
Above the dark *Upsaras* [1] flew, beneath us plashed
the blood,
And, bellying black against the dust, the Bhagwa
Jhanda swayed.

I saw it fall in smoke and fire, the banner of the
Bhao ;
I heard a voice across the press of one who called
in vain :—

[1] The Choosers of the Slain.

'Ho! Anand Rao Nimbalkhur, ride! Get aid of
  Mulhar Rao!
  'Go shame his squadrons into fight—the Bhao—
    the Bhao is slain!'

Thereat, as when a sand-bar breaks in clotted spume
    and spray—
  When rain of later autumn sweeps the Jumna
    water-head,
Before their charge from flank to flank our riven
    ranks gave way;
  But of the waters of that flood the Jumna fords
    ran red.

I held by Scindia, my lord, as close as man might
    hold;
  A Soobah of the Deccan asks no aid to guard his
    life;
But Holkar's Horse were flying, and our chiefest
    chiefs were cold,
  And like a flame among us leapt the long lean
    Northern knife.

I held by Scindia—my lance from butt to tuft was
     dyed,
  The froth of battle bossed the shield and roped
     the bridle-chain—
What time beneath our horses' feet a maiden rose
     and cried,
  And clung to Scindia, and I turned a sword-cut
     from the twain.

(He set a spell upon the maid in woodlands
     long ago,
  A hunter by the Tapti banks she gave him water
     there :
He turned her heart to water, and she followed to
     her woe.
  What need had he of Lalun who had twenty
     maids as fair ?)

Now in that hour strength left my lord : he wrenched
     his mare aside ;
  He bound the girl behind him and we slashed and
     struggled free.

Across the reeling wreck of strife we rode as shadows
    ride
  From Paniput to Delhi town, but not alone
    were we.

'Twas Lutuf-Ullah Populzai laid horse upon our
    track,
  A swine-fed reiver of the North that lusted for the
    maid ;
I might have barred his path awhile, but Scindia
    called me back,
  And I—O woe for Scindia !—I listened and
    obeyed.

League after league the formless scrub took shape
    and glided by—
  League after league the white road swirled behind
    the white mare's feet—
League after league, when leagues were done, we
    heard the Populzai,
  Where sure as Time and swift as Death the tireless
    footfall beat.

Noon's eye beheld that shame of flight, the shadows
fell, we fled
Where steadfast as the wheeling kite he followed
in our train ;
The black wolf warred where we had warred, the
jackal mocked our dead,
And terror born of twilight-tide made mad the
labouring brain.

I gasped :—' A kingdom waits my lord ; her love is
but her own.
' A day shall mar, a day shall cure for her, but what
for thee ?
' Cut loose the girl : he follows fast.   Cut loose and
ride alone ! '
Then Scindia 'twixt his blistered lips :—' My
Queens' Queen shall she be !

' Of all who ate my bread last night 'twas she alone
that came
' To seek her love between the spears and find her
crown therein !

' One shame is mine to-day, what need the weight of
    double shame ?

    ' If once we reach the Delhi gate, though all be
        lost, I win ! '

We rode—the white mare failed—her trot a stagger-
    ing stumble grew,—

    The cooking-smoke of even rose and weltered and
        hung low ;

And still we heard the Populzai and still we strained
    anew,

    And Delhi town was very near. but nearer was
        the foe.

Yea, Delhi town was very near when Lalun whispered :
    ' Slay !

    ' Lord of my life, the mare sinks fast—stab deep
        and let me die ! '

But Scindia would not, and the maid tore free and
    flung away,

    And turning as she fell we heard the clattering
        Populzai.

Then Scindia checked the gasping mare that rocked
    and groaned for breath,
  And wheeled to charge and plunged the knife a
    handsbreadth in her side—
The hunter and the hunted know how that last pause
    is death—
  The blood had chilled about her heart, she reared
    and fell and died

Our Gods were kind.   Before he heard the maiden's
    piteous scream
  A log upon the Delhi road, beneath the mare he
    lay—
Lost mistress and lost battle passed before him like
    a dream ;
  The darkness closed about his eyes—I bore my
    King away.

THE BALLAD OF BOH DA THONE

This is the ballad of Boh Da Thone,
Erst a Pretender to Theebaw's throne,
Who harried the district of Alalone :
How he met with his fate and the V.P.P
At the hand of Harendra Mukerji,
Senior Gomashta, G.B.T.

BOH DA THONE was a warrior bold :
His sword and his Snider were bossed with gold.

And the Peacock Banner his henchmen bore
Was stiff with bullion, but stiffer with gore.

He shot at the strong and he slashed at the weak
From the Salween scrub to the Chindwin teak :

He crucified noble, he sacrificed mean,
He filled old ladies with kerosene :

While over the water the papers cried,
' The patriot fights for his countryside ! '

112

But little they cared for the Native Press,
The worn white soldiers in Khaki dress,

Who tramped through the jungle and camped in
the byre,
Who died in the swamp and were tombed in the
mire,

Who gave up their lives, at the Queen's Command,
For the Pride of their Race and the Peace of the
Land.

Now, first of the foemen of Boh Da Thone
Was Captain O'Neil of the ' Black Tyrone,'

And his was a Company, seventy strong,
Who hustled that dissolute Chief along.

There were lads from Galway and Louth and
Meath
Who went to their death with a joke in their teeth,

And worshipped with fluency, fervour, and zeal
The mud on the boot-heels of ' Crook ' O'Neil.

But ever a blight on their labours lay,
And ever their quarry would vanish away,

H

Till the sun-dried boys of the Black Tyrone
Took a brotherly interest in Boh Da Thone :

And, sooth, if pursuit in possession ends,
The Boh and his trackers were best of friends.

The word of a scout—a march by night—
A rush through the mist—a scattering fight—

A volley from cover—a corpse in the clearing—
The glimpse of a loin-cloth and heavy jade earring—

The flare of a village—the tally of slain—
And . . . the Boh was abroad ' on the raid ' again !

They cursed their luck, as the Irish will,
They gave him credit for cunning and skill,

They buried their dead, they bolted their beef,
And started anew on the track of the thief,

Till, in place of the ' Kalends of Greece,' men said,
' When Crook and his darlings come back with the
    head.'

They had hunted the Boh from the hills to the
    plain—
He doubled and broke for the hills again :

They had crippled his power for rapine and raid,
They had routed him out of his pet stockade,

And at last, they came, when the Day Star tired.
To a camp deserted—a village fired.

A black cross blistered the Morning-gold,
And the body upon it was stark and cold.

The wind of the dawn went merrily past,
The high grass bowed her plumes to the blast

And out of the grass, on a sudden, broke
A spirtle of fire, a whorl of smoke—

And Captain O'Neil of the Black Tyrone
Was blessed with a slug in the ulnar-bone—
The gift of his enemy Boh Da Thone.

(Now a slug that is hammered from telegraph-wire
Is a thorn in the flesh and a rankling fire.)

.   .   .   .

The shot-wound festered—as shot-wounds may
In a steaming barrack at Mandalay.

The left arm throbbed, and the Captain swore,
' I 'd like to be after the Boh once more ! '

The fever held him—the Captain said,
' I 'd give a hundred to look at his head ! '

The Hospital punkahs creaked and whirred,
But Babu Harendra (Gomashta) heard.

He thought of the cane-brake, green and dank,
That girdled his home by the Dacca tank.

He thought of his wife and his High School son,
He thought—but abandoned the thought—of a gun

His sleep was broken by visions dread
Of a shining Boh with a silver head.

He kept his counsel and went his way,
And swindled the cartmen of half their pay.

.   .   .   .

And the months went on, as the worst must do
And the Boh returned to the raid anew.

But the Captain had quitted the long-drawn strife,
And in far Simoorie had taken a wife.

And she was a damsel of delicate mould,
With hair like the sunshine and heart of gold,

And little she knew the arms that embraced
Had cloven a man from the brow to the waist :

And little she knew that the loving lips
Had ordered a quivering life's eclipse,

And the eye that lit at her lightest breath
Had glared unawed in the Gates of Death.

(For these be matters a man would hide,
As a general rule, from an innocent Bride.)

And little the Captain thought of the past,
And, of all men, Babu Harendra last.

.   .   .   .

But slow, in the sludge of the Kathun road,
The Government Bullock Train toted its load.

Speckless and spotless and shining with *ghee.*
In the rearmost cart sat the Babu-jee.

And ever a phantom before him fled
Of a scowling Boh with a silver head.

Then the lead-cart stuck, though the coolies slaved,
And the cartmen flogged and the escort raved ;

And out of the jungle, with yells and squeals,
Pranced Boh Da Thone, and his gang at his heels !

Then belching blunderbuss answered back
The Snider's snarl and the carbine's crack,

And the blithe revolver began to sing
To the blade that twanged on the locking-ring,

And the brown flesh blued where the bay'net
    kissed,
As the steel shot back with a wrench and a twist,

And the great white bullocks with onyx eyes
Watched the souls of the dead arise,

And over the smoke of the fusillade
The Peacock Banner staggered and swayed

Oh, gayest of scrimmages man may see
Is a well-worked rush on the G.B.T. !

The Babu shook at the horrible sight,
And girded his ponderous loins for flight,

But Fate had ordained that the Boh should start
On a lone-hand raid of the rearmost cart,

And out of that cart, with a bellow of woe,
The Babu fell—flat on the top of the Boh !

For years had Harendra served the State,
To the growth of his purse and the girth of his
    pêt.

There were twenty stone, as the tally-man knows,
On the broad of the chest of this best of Bohs.

And twenty stone from a height discharged
Are bad for a Boh with a spleen enlarged.

Oh, short was the struggle—severe was the shock—
He dropped like a bullock—he lay like a block ;

And the Babu above him, convulsed with fear,
Heard the labouring life-breath hissed out in his
    ear.

And thus in a fashion undignified
The princely pest of the Chindwin died

.   .   .   .

Turn now to Simoorie where, lapped in his ease,
The Captain is petting the Bride on his knees,

Where the *whit* of the bullet, the wounded man's
    scream
Are mixed as the mist of some devilish dream—

Forgotten, forgotten the sweat of the shambles
Where the hill-daisy blooms and the grey monkey
    gambols,

From the sword-belt set free and released from the
    steel,
The Peace of the Lord is with Captain O'Neil.

Up the hill to Simoorie—most patient of drudges—
The bags on his shoulder, the mail-runner trudges.

' For Captain O'Neil, *Sahib*.   One hundred and ten
' Rupees to collect on delivery.'

                            Then
(Their breakfast was stopped while the screw-jack
    and hammer
Tore waxcloth, split teak-wood, and chipped out
    the dammer ;)

Open-eyed, open-mouthed, on the napery's snow,
With a crash and a thud, rolled—the Head of the
    Boh !

And gummed to the scalp was a letter which
    ran :—

' In Fielding Force Service.

' *Encampment,*

' 10th Jan.

' Dear Sir,—I have honour to send, *as you said,*
' For final approval (see under) Boh's Head ;

' Was took by myself in most bloody affair.
' By High Education brought pressure to bear.

' Now violate Liberty, time being bad,
' To mail V.P.P. (rupees hundred) Please add

' Whatever Your Honour can pass.   Price of Blood
' Much cheap at one hundred, and children want food;

' So trusting Your Honour will somewhat retain
' True love and affection for Govt. Bullock Train,

' And show awful kindness to satisfy me,
       ' I am,

          ' Graceful Master,

             ' Your

                ' H. Mukerji.

•   •   •   •   •   •   •   •   •

As the rabbit is drawn to the rattlesnake's power.
As the smoker's eye fills at the opium hour,

As a horse reaches up to the manger above,
As the waiting ear yearns for the whisper of love.

From the arms of the Bride, iron-visaged and slow.
The Captain bent down to the Head of the Boh.

And e'en as he looked on the Thing where It lay
'Twixt the winking new spoons and the napkins'
   array,

The freed mind fled back to the long-ago days—
The hand-to-hand scuffle—the smoke and the
   blaze—

The forced march at night and the quick rush at
   dawn—
The banjo at twilight, the burial ere morn—

The stench of the marshes—the raw, piercing smell
When the overhand stabbing-cut silenced the yell—

The oaths of his Irish that surged when they stood
Where the black crosses hung o'er the Kuttamow
   flood.

As a derelict ship drifts away with the tide
The Captain went out on the Past from his Bride,

Back, back, through the springs to the chill of the
    year,
When he hunted the Boh from Maloon to Tsaleer.

As the shape of a corpse dimmers up through deep
    water,
In his eye lit the passionless passion of slaughter,

And men who had fought with O'Neil for the life
Had gazed on his face with less dread than his wife.

For she who had held him so long could not hold
    him—
Though a four-month Eternity should have con
    trolled him—

But watched the twin Terror—the head turned to
    head—
The scowling, scarred Black, and the flushed savage
    Red—

The spirit that changed from her knowing and
    flew to
Some grim hidden Past she had never a clue to.

But It knew as It grinned, for he touched it un-
    fearing,
And muttered aloud, ' So you kept that jade ear-
    ring ! '

Then nodded, and kindly, as friend nods to friend,
' Old man, you fought well, but you lost in the end.'

   .   .   .   .

The visions departed, and Shame followed Passion :—
' He took what I said in this horrible fashion,

' *I 'll* write to Harendra ! '   With language unsainted
The Captain came back to the Bride . . . who had
    fainted.

   .   .   .   .

And this is a fiction ?   No.   Go to Simoorie
And look at their baby, a twelve-month old Houri,

A pert little, Irish-eyed Kathleen Mavournin—
She 's always about on the Mall of a mornin'—

And you 'll see, if her right shoulder-strap is dis-
    placed,
This : *Gules* upon *argent*, a Boh's Head, *erased !*

THE LAMENT OF THE BORDER CATTLE
THIEF

O woe is me for the merry life
    I led beyond the Bar,
And a treble woe for my winsome wife
    That weeps at Shalimar.

They have taken away my long jezail,
    My shield and sabre fine,
And heaved me into the Central Jail
    For lifting of the kine.

The steer may low within the byre,
    The Jut may tend his grain,
But there 'll be neither loot nor fire
    Till I come back again.

And God have mercy on the Jut
    When once my fetters fall,
And Heaven defend the farmer's hut
    When I am loosed from thrall.

It 's woe to bend the stubborn back
    Above the grinching quern,
It 's woe to hear the leg-bar clack
    And jingle when I turn !

But for the sorrow and the shame.
    The brand on me and mine,
I 'll pay you back in leaping flame.
    And loss of the butchered kine.

For every cow I spared before
    In charity set free,
If I may reach my hold once more
    I 'll reive an honest three.

For every time I raised the lowe
    That scared the dusty plain,
By sword and cord, by torch and tow
    I 'll light the land with twain.

Ride hard, ride hard to Abazai,
    Young *Sahib* with the yellow hair—
Lie close, lie close as khuttucks lie,
    Fat herds below Bonair.

The one I 'll shoot at twilight-tide,
 At dawn I 'll drive the other ;
The black shall mourn for hoof and hide,
 The white man for his brother.

'Tis war, red war, I 'll give you then,
 War till my sinews fail ;
For the wrong you have done to a chief of men
 And a thief of the Zukka Khey.

And if I fall to your hand afresh
 I give you leave for the sin,
That you cram my throat with the foul pig's flesh.
 And swing me in the skin !

THE RHYME OF THE THREE CAPTAINS

This ballad appears to refer to one of the exploits of the notorious Paul Jones, the American pirate. It is founded on fact.

. . . At the close of a winter day,
Their anchors down, by London town, the Three
    Great Captains lay :
And one was Admiral of the North from Solway
    Firth to Skye,
And one was Lord of the Wessex coast and all the
    lands thereby,
And one was Master of the Thames from Limehouse
    to Blackwall,
And he was Captain of the Fleet—the bravest of
    them all.
Their good guns guarded the great grey sides that
    were thirty foot in the sheer,
When there came a certain trading brig with news
    of a privateer.

Her rigging was rough with the clotted drift that
    drives in a Northern breeze,
Her sides were clogged with the lazy weed that
    spawns in the Eastern seas.
Light she rode in the rude tide-rip, to left and right
    she rolled,
And the skipper sat on the scuttle-butt and stared
    at an empty hold.
'I ha' paid Port dues for your Law,' quoth he, ' and
    where is the Law ye boast
' If I sail unscathed from a heathen port to be robbed
    on a Christian coast ?
' Ye have smoked the hives of the Laccadives as we
    burn the lice in a bunk,
' We tack not now to a Gallang prow or a plunging
    Pei-ho junk ;
' I had no fear but the seas were clear as far as a sail
    might fare
' Till I met with a lime-washed Yankee brig that rode
    off Finisterre.
' There were canvas blinds to his bow-gun ports to
    screen the weight he bore,
' And the signals ran for a merchantman from Sandy
    Hook to the Nore.

' He would not fly the Rovers' flag—the bloody o۱
    the black,
' But now he floated the Gridiron and now he flaunted
    the Jack.
' He spoke of the Law as he crimped my crew—he
    swore it was only a loan ;
˙ But when I would ask for my own again, he swore
    it was none of my own.
˙ He has taken my little parrakeets that nest beneath
    the Line,
  He has stripped my rails of the shaddock-trails and
    the green unripened pine ;
  He has taken my bale of dammer and spice I won
    beyond the seas,
˙ He has taken my grinning heathen gods—and what
    should he want o' these ?
˙ My foremast would not mend his boom, my deck-
    house patch his boats ;
  He has whittled the two, this Yank Yahoo, to peddle
    for shoe-peg oats
˙ I could not fight for the failing light and a rough
    beam-sea beside,
˙ But I hulled him once for a clumsy crimp and twice
    because he lied.

'Had I had guns (as I had goods) to work my
  Christian harm,
'I had run him up from his quarter-deck to trade
  with his own yard-arm ;
'I had nailed his ears to my capstan-head, and ripped
  them off with a saw,
And soused them in the bilgewater, and served them
  to him raw ;
'I had flung him blind in a rudderless boat to rot in
  the rocking dark,
I had towed him aft of his own craft, a bait for his
  brother shark ;
I had lapped him round with cocoa husk. and
  drenched him with the oil,
'And lashed him fast to his own mast to blaze above
  my spoil ;
'I had stripped his hide for my hammock-side, and
  tasselled his beard i' the mesh,
'And spitted his crew on the live bamboo that grows
  through the gangrened flesh :
'I had hove him down by the mangroves brown,
  where the mud-reef sucks and draws,
'Moored by the heel to his own keel to wait for the
  land-crab's claws !

' He is lazar within and lime without, ye can nose
     him far enow,

' For he carries the taint of a musky ship—the reek
     of the slaver's dhow ! '

The skipper looked at the tiering guns and the
     bulwarks tall and cold,

And the Captains Three full courteously peered
     down at the gutted hold,

And the Captains Three called courteously from
     deck to scuttle-butt :—

' Good Sir, we ha' dealt with that merchantman or
     ever your teeth were cut.

' Your words be words of a lawless race, and the Law
     it standeth thus :

' He comes of a race that have never a Law, and he
     never has boarded us.

' We ha' sold him canvas and rope and spar—we
     know that his price is fair,

' And we know that he weeps for the lack of a Law
     as he rides off Finisterre.

' And since he is damned for a gallows-thief by you
     and better than you,

' We hold it meet that the English fleet should know
     that we hold him true.'

The skipper called to the tall taffrail :—' And what
    is that to me ?

' Did ever you hear of a Yankee brig that rifled a
    Seventy-three ?

' Do I loom so large from your quarter-deck that I
    lift like a ship o' the Line ?

' He has learned to run from a shotted gun and harry
    such craft as mine.

' There is never a Law on the Cocos Keys to hold
    a white man in,

' But we do not steal the niggers meal, for that is a
    nigger's sin.

' Must he have his Law as a quid to chaw, or laid in
    brass on his wheel ?

' Does he steal with tears when he buccaneers ?
    'Fore Gad, then, why does he steal ? '

The skipper bit on a deep-sea word, and the word
    it was not sweet,

For he could see the Captains Three had signalled
    to the Fleet.

But three and two, in white and blue, the whimpering
    flags began :—

' We have heard a tale of a—foreign sail, but he is
    a merchantman.'

The skipper peered beneath his palm and swore by
    the Great Horn Spoon :—

' 'Fore Gad, the Chaplain of the Fleet would bless
    my picaroon ! '

By two and three the flags blew free to lash the
    laughing air :—

' We have sold our spars to the merchantman—we
    know that his price is fair.'

The skipper winked his Western eye, and swore by
    a China storm :—

' They ha' rigged him a Joseph's jury-coat to keep
    his honour warm.'

The halliards twanged against the tops, the bunting
    bellied broad,

The skipper spat in the empty hold and mourned
    for a wasted cord.

Masthead—masthead, the signal sped by the line
    o' the British craft :

The skipper called to his Lascar crew, and put her
    about and laughed :—

' It 's mainsail haul, my bully boys all—we 'll out to
    the seas again—

' Ere they set us to paint their pirate saint, or scrub
    at his grapnel-chain.

' It 's fore-sheet free, with her head to the sea, and
 the swing of the unbought brine—

' We 'll make no sport in an English court till we
 come as a ship o' the Line :

' Till we come as a ship o' the Line, my lads, of
 thirty foot in the sheer,

' Lifting again from the outer main with news of a
 privateer ;

' Flying his pluck at our mizzen-truck for weft of
 Admiralty,

' Heaving his head for our dipsy-lead in sign that we
 keep the sea.

' Then fore-sheet home as she lifts to the foam—we
 stand on the outward tack,

' We are paid in the coin of the white man's trade—
 the bezant is hard, ay, and black.

' The frigate-bird shall carry my word to the Kling
 and the Orang-Laut

' How a man may sail from a heathen coast to be
 robbed in a Christian port ;

' How a man may be robbed in Christian port while
 Three Great Captains there

' Shall dip their flag to a slaver's rag—to show that
 his trade is fair ! '

THE BALLAD OF THE ' CLAMPHERDOWN

IT was our war-ship ' Clampherdown '
  Would sweep the Channel clean,
Wherefore she kept her hatches close
When the merry Channel chops arose.
  To save the bleached marine.

She had one bow-gun of a hundred ton.
  And a great stern-gun beside ;
They dipped their noses deep in the sea.
They racked their stays and stanchions free
  In the wash of the wind-whipped tide

It was our war-ship ' Clampherdown '
  Fell in with a cruiser light
That carried the dainty Hotchkiss gun
And a pair o' heels wherewith to run
  From the grip of a close-fought fight.

She opened fire at seven miles—
   As ye shoot at a bobbing cork—
And once she fired and twice she fired,
Till the bow-gun drooped like a lily tired
   That lolls upon the stalk.

' Captain, the bow-gun melts apace,
   ' The deck-beams break below,
" 'Twere well to rest for an hour or twain,
' And botch the shattered plates again.'
   And he answered, ' Make it so.'

She opened fire within the mile—
   As ye shoot at the flying duck—
And the great stern-gun shot fair and true,
With the heave of the ship, to the stainless
      blue,
   And the great stern-turret stuck.

' Captain, the turret fills with steam,
   ' The feed-pipes burst below—
' You can hear the hiss of the helpless ram.
' You can hear the twisted runners jam.'
   And he answered, ' Turn and go ! '

It was our war-ship ' Clampherdown,'
   And grimly did she roll ;
Swung round to take the cruiser's fire
As the White Whale faces the Thresher's ire
   When they war by the frozen Pole.

' Captain, the shells are falling fast,
  ' And faster still fall we ;
' And it is not meet for English stock
To bide in the heart of an eight-day ciock
   The death they cannot see.'

' Lie down, lie down, my bold A.B.,
  ' We drift upon her beam ;
' We dare not ram, for she can run ,
' And dare ye fire another gun,
  ' And die in the peeling steam ? '

It was our war-ship ' Clampherdown
   That carried an armour-belt ;
But fifty feet at stern and bow
Lay bare as the paunch of the purser's sow
   To the hail of the Nordenfeldt.

' Captain, they hack us through and through ;
  ' The chilled steel bolts are swift !
' We have emptied the bunkers in open sea,
' Their shrapnel bursts where our coal should be '
  And he answered, ' Let her drift.'

It was our war-ship ' Clampherdown,'
  Swung round upon the tide,
Her two dumb guns glared south and north,
And the blood and the bubbling steam ran forth,
  And she ground the cruiser's side.

' Captain, they cry, the fight is done,
  ' They bid you send your sword.'
And he answered, ' Grapple her stern and bow.
' They have asked for the steel.   They shall have it
      now ;
  ' Out cutlasses and board ! '

It was our war-ship ' Clampherdown
  Spewed up four hundred men ;
And the scalded stokers yelped delight,
As they rolled in the waist and heard the fight,
  Stamp o'er their steel-walled pen.

They cleared the cruiser end to end,
   From conning-tower to hold.
They fought as they fought in Nelson's fleet ;
They were stripped to the waist, they were bare
      to the feet,
   As it was in the days of old.

It was the sinking ' Clampherdown '
   Heaved up her battered side—
And carried a million pounds in steel,
To the cod and the corpse-fed conger-eel,
   And the scour of the Channel tide.

It was the crew of the ' Clampherdown '
   Stood out to sweep the sea,
On a cruiser won from an ancient foe
As it was in the days of long ago.
   And as it still shall be

THE BALLAD OF THE BOLIVAR·

Seven men from all the world back to Docks again,
Rolling down the Ratcliffe Road drunk and raising
  Cain :
Give the girls another drink 'fore we sign away—
We that took the ' Bolivar ' out across the Bay !

WE put out from Sunderland loaded down with
  rails ;
  We put back to Sunderland 'cause our cargo
  shifted ;
We put out from Sunderland—met the winter
  gales—
  Seven days and seven nights to the Start we
  drifted.

  Racketing her rivets loose, smoke-stack white
  as snow,
  All the coals adrift adeck, half the rails below

Leaking like a lobster-pot, steering like a dray—
Out we took the ' Bolivar,' out across the Bay !

One by one the Lights came up, winked and let us by ;
Mile by mile we waddled on, coal and fo'c'sle short ;
Met a blow that laid us down, heard a bulkhead fly ;
Left the ' Wolf ' behind us with a two-foot list to port.

Trailing like a wounded duck, working out her soul ;
Clanging like a smithy-shop after every roll ;
Just a funnel and a mast lurching through the spray—
So we threshed the ' Bolivar ' out across the Bay !

Felt her hog and felt her sag, betted when she 'd break ;
Wondered every time she raced if she 'd stand the shock ;

Heard the seas like drunken men pounding at her
    strake ;
  Hoped the Lord 'ud keep his thumb on the
    plummer-block.

    Banged against the iron decks, bilges choked
      with coal ;
    Flayed and frozen foot and hand, sick of heart
      and soul ;
    Last we prayed she 's buck herself into Judg-
      ment Day—
    Hi ! we cursed the ' Bolivar ' knocking round
      the Bay !

O her nose flung up to sky, groaning to be still—
  Up and down and back we went, never time for
    breath ;
Then the money paid at Lloyd's caught her by the
    heel,
  And the stars ran round and round dancin' at our
    death.

    Aching for an hour's sleep, dozing off between ;
    Heard the rotten rivets draw when she took it
      green ;

Watched the compass chase its tail like a cat at
play—
That was on the ' Bolivar,' south across the Bay.

Once we saw between the squalls, lyin' head to
swell—
Mad with work and weariness, wishin' they was
we—
Some damned Liner's lights go by like a grand
hotel ;
Cheered her from the ' Bolivar ' swampin' in
the sea.

Then a greyback cleared us out, then the
skipper laughed ;
' Boys, the wheel has gone to Hell—rig the
winches aft !
' Yoke the kicking rudder-head—get her under
way ! '
So we steered her, pully-haul, out across the
Bay !

Just a pack o' rotten plates puttied up with tar,
In we came, an' time enough, 'cross Bilbao Bar.

Overloaded, undermanned, meant to founder, we
Euchred God Almighty's storm, bluffed the Eternal Sea!

Seven men from all the world, back to town again,
Rollin' down the Ratcliffe Road drunk and raising Cain :
Seven men from out of Hell. Ain't the owners gay,
Cause we took the ' Bolivar ' safe across the Bay ?

K

THE SACRIFICE OF ER-HEB

Er-Heb beyond the Hills of Ao-Safai
Bears witness to the truth, and Ao-Safai
Hath told the men of Gorukh.   Thence the tale
Comes westward o'er the peaks to India.

The story of Bisesa, Armod's child,—
A maiden plighted to the Chief in War,
The Man of Sixty Spears, who held the Pass
That leads to Thibet, but to-day is gone
To seek his comfort of the God called Budh
The Silent—showing how the Sickness ceased
Because of her who died to save the tribe.

Taman is One and greater than us all,
Taman is One and greater than all Gods :
Taman is Two in One and rides the sky,
Curved like a stallion's croup, from dusk to dawn,
And drums upon it with his heels, whereby
Is bred the neighing thunder in the hills.

This is Taman, the God of all Er-Heb,
Who was before all Gods, and made all Gods,
And presently will break the Gods he made,
And step upon the Earth to govern men
Who give him milk-dry ewes and cheat his
    Priests,
Or leave his shrine unlighted—as Er-Heb
Left it unlighted and forgot Taman,
When all the Valley followed after Kysh
And Yabosh, little Gods but very wise,
And from the sky Taman beheld their sin.

He sent the Sickness out upon the hills,
The Red Horse Sickness with the iron hooves,
To turn the Valley to Taman again.

And the Red Horse snuffed thrice into the wind,
The naked wind that had no fear of him ;
And the Red Horse stamped thrice upon the snow,
The naked snow that had no fear of him ;
And the Red Horse went out across the rocks,
The ringing rocks that had no fear of him ;
And downward, where the lean birch meets the
    snow,

And downward, where the grey pine meets the birch,
And downward, where the dwarf oak meets the pine,
Till at his feet our cup-like pastures lay.

That night, the slow mists of the evening dropped,
Dropped as a cloth upon a dead man's face,
And weltered in the valley, bluish-white
Like water very silent—spread abroad,
Like water very silent, from the Shrine
Unlighted of Taman to where the stream
Is dammed to fill our cattle-troughs—sent up
White waves that rocked and heaved and then were
        still,
Till all the Valley glittered like a marsh,
Beneath the moonlight, filled with sluggish mist
Knee-deep, so that men waded as they walked.

That night, the Red Horse grazed above the Dam.
Beyond the cattle-troughs.   Men heard him feed,
And those that heard him sickened where they lay

Thus came the sickness to Er-Heb, and slew
Ten men, strong men, and of the women four ;
And the Red Horse went hillward with the dawn,
But near the cattle-troughs his hoof-prints lay.

That night, the slow mists of the evening dropped,
Dropped as a cloth upon the dead, but rose
A little higher, to a young girl's height ;
Till all the valley glittered like a lake,
Beneath the moonlight, filled with sluggish mist.

That night, the Red Horse grazed beyond the Dam
A stone's-throw from the troughs.   Men heard him
    feed,
And those that heard him sickened where they lay,
Thus came the sickness to Er-Heb, and slew
Of men a score, and of the women eight,
And of the children two.

                Because the road
To Gorukh was a road of enemies,
And Ao-Safai was blocked with early snow,
We could not flee from out the Valley.   Death
Smote at us in a slaughter-pen, and Kysh
Was mute as Yabosh, though the goats were slain ;
And the Red Horse grazed nightly by the stream,
And later, outward, towards the Unlighted Shrine,
And those that heard him sickened where they
    lay.

Then said Bisesa to the Priests at dusk,
When the white mist rose up breast-high, and choked
The voices in the houses of the dead :—
' Yabosh and Kysh avail not.   If the Horse
' Reach the Unlighted Shrine we surely die.
' Ye have forgotten of all Gods the chief,
' Taman !'   Here rolled the thunder through the Hill
And Yabosh shook upon his pedestal.
' Ye have forgotten of all Gods the chief
' Too long.'   And all were dumb save one, who cried
On Yabosh with the Sapphire 'twixt His knees,
But found no answer in the smoky roof,
And, being smitten of the sickness, died
Before the altar of the Sapphire Shrine.

Then said Bisesa :—' I am near to Death,
' And have the Wisdom of the Grave for gift
' To bear me on the path my feet must tread.
' If there be wealth on earth, then I am rich,
' For Armod is the first of all Er-Heb ;
' If there be beauty on the earth,'—her eyes
Dropped for a moment to the temple floor,—
' Ye know that I am fair.   If there be Love,
' Ye know that love is mine.'   The Chief in War,

The Man of Sixty Spears, broke from the press,
And would have clasped her, but the Priests with·
    stood,
Saying :—' She has a message from Taman.'
Then said Bisesa :—' By my wealth and love
' And beauty, I am chosen of the God
' Taman.'   Here rolled the thunder through the
    Hills
And Kysh fell forward on the Mound of Skulls.

In darkness, and before our Priests, the maid
Between the altars cast her bracelets down,
Therewith the heavy earrings Armod made,
When he was young, out of the water-gold
Of Gorukh—threw the breast-plate thick with jade
Upon the turquoise anklets—put aside
The bands of silver on her brow and neck ;
And as the trinkets tinkled on the stones,
The thunder of Taman lowed like a bull.

Then said Bisesa, stretching out her hands,
As one in darkness fearing Devils :—' Help !
' O Priests, I am a woman very weak.

' And who am I to know the will of Gods ?
' Taman hath called me—whither shall I go ? '
The Chief in War, the Man of Sixty Spears,
Howled in his torment, fettered by the Priests,
But dared not come to her to drag her forth,
And dared not lift his spear against the Priests
Then all men wept.

                 There was a Priest of Kysh
Bent with a hundred winters, hairless, blind,
And taloned as the great Snow-Eagle is.
His seat was nearest to the altar-fires,
And he was counted dumb among the Priests.
But, whether Kysh decreed, or from Taman
The impotent tongue found utterance we know
As little as the bats beneath the eaves.
He cried so that they heard who stood without :—
' To the Unlighted Shrine ! ' and crept aside
Into the shadow of his fallen God
And whimpered, and Bisesa went her way.

That night, the slow mists of the evening dropped.
Dropped as a cloth upon the dead, and rose
Above the roofs, and by the Unlighted Shrine

Lay as the slimy water of the troughs
When murrain thins the cattle of Er-Heb :
And through the mist men heard the Red Horse
    feed.

In Armod's house they burned Bisesa's dower,
And killed her black bull Tor, and broke her wheel,
And loosed her hair, as for the marriage-feast,
With cries more loud than mourning for the dead.

Across the fields, from Armod's dwelling-place,
We heard Bisesa weeping where she passed
To seek the Unlighted Shrine ; the Red Horse
    neighed
And followed her, and on the river-mint
His hooves struck dead and heavy in our ears.

Out of the mists of evening, as the star
Of Ao-Safai climbs through the black snow-blur
To show the Pass is clear, Bisesa stepped
Upon the great grey slope of mortised stone,
The Causeway of Taman. The Red Horse neighed
Behind her to the Unlighted Shrine—then fled
North to the Mountain where his stable lies.

They know who dared the anger of Taman,
And watched that night above the clinging mists
Far up the hill, Bisesa's passing in.

She set her hand upon the carven door,
Fouled by a myriad bats, and black with time,
Whereon is graved the Glory of Taman
In letters older than the Ao-Safai ;
And twice she turned aside and twice she wept
Cast down upon the threshold, clamouring
For him she loved—the Man of Sixty Spears,
And for her father,—and the black bull Tor,
Hers and her pride.   Yea, twice she turned away
Before the awful darkness of the door,
And the great horror of the Wall of Man
Where Man is made the plaything of Taman,
An Eyeless Face that waits above and laughs.

But the third time she cried and put her palms
Against the hewn stone leaves, and prayed Taman
To spare Er-Heb and take her life for price.

They know who watched, the doors were rent apart
And closed upon Bisesa, and the rain

Broke like a flood across the Valley, washed
The mist away ; but louder than the rain
The thunder of Taman filled men with fear.

Some say that from the Unlighted Shrine she cried
For succour, very pitifully, thrice,
And others that she sang and had no fear.
And some that there was neither song nor cry,
But only thunder and the lashing rain.

Howbeit, in the morning men rose up,
Perplexed with horror, crowding to the Shrine,
And when Er-Heb was gathered at the doors
The Priests made lamentation and passed in
To a strange Temple and a God they feared
But knew not

          From the crevices the grass
Had thrust the altar-slabs apart, the walls
Were grey with stains unclean, the roof-beams
    swelled
With many-coloured growth of rottenness,
And lichen veiled the Image of Taman
In leprosy.   The Basin of the Blood

Above the altar held the morning sun :
A winking ruby on its heart : below,
Face hid in hands, the maid Bisesa lay

Er-Heb beyond the Hills of Ao-Safai
Bears witness to the truth, and Ao-Safai
Hath told the men of Gorukh.   Thence the tale
Comes westward o'er the peaks to India.

THE EXPLANATION

Love and Death once ceased their strife
At the Tavern of Man's Life.
Called for wine, and threw—alas !—
Each his quiver on the grass.
When the bout was o'er they found
Mingled arrows strewed the ground.
Hastily they gathered then
Each the loves and lives of men.
Ah, the fateful dawn deceived !
Mingled arrows each one sheaved :
Death's dread armoury was stored
With the shafts he most abhorred ;
Love's light quiver groaned beneath
Venom-headed darts of Death.

Thus it was they wrought our woe
At the Tavern long ago.
Tell me, do our masters know,
Loosing blindly as they fly,
Old men love while young men die ?

THE GIFT OF THE SEA

THE dead child lay in the shroud,
　　And the widow watched beside ;
And her mother slept, and the Channel swept
　　The gale in the teeth of the tide.

But the mother laughed at all.
　　' I have lost my man in the sea,
And the child is dead.　Be still,' she said,
　　' What more can ye do to me ? '

The widow watched the dead,
　　And the candle guttered low,
And she tried to sing the Passing Song
　　That bids the poor soul go.

And ' Mary take you now,' she sang,
　　' That lay against my heart.'
And ' Mary smooth your crib to-night,
　　But she could not say ' Depart.'

Then came a cry from the sea,
  But the sea-rime blinded the glass,
And ' Heard ye nothing, mother ? ' she said
  · 'Tis the child that waits to pass.'

And the nodding mother sighed.
  ' 'Tis a lambing ewe in the whin,
' For why should the christened soul cry out
  ' That never knew of sin ? '

' O feet I have held in my hand,
  ' O hands at my heart to catch,
' How should they know the road to go,
  ' And how should they lift the latch ? '

They laid a sheet to the door,
  With the little quilt atop,
That it might not hurt from the cold or the dirt
  But the crying would not stop.

The widow lifted the latch
  And strained her eyes to see,
And opened the door on the bitter shore
  To let the soul go free.

There was neither glimmer nor ghost,
  There was neither spirit nor spark,
And ' Heard ye nothing, mother ? ' she said
  ' 'Tis crying for me in the dark.'

And the nodding mother sighed :
  ' 'Tis sorrow makes ye dull ;
' Have ye yet to learn the cry of the tern,
  ' Or the wail of the wind-blown gull ?

' The terns are blown inland,
  ' The grey gull follows the plough.
' 'Twas never a bird, the voice I heard,
    O mother, I hear it now ! '

Lie still, dear lamb, lie still ;
  ' The child is passed from harm,
Tis the ache in your breast that broke your rest
  ' And the feel of an empty arm.'

She put her mother aside,
  ' In Mary's name let be !
For the peace of my soul I must go,' she said,
  And she went to the calling sea.

In the heel of the wind-bit pier,
  Where the twisted weed was piled,
She came to the life she had missed by an hour,
  For she came to a little child.

She laid it into her breast,
  And back to her mother she came,
But it would not feed and it would not heed,
  Though she gave it her own child's name.

And the dead child dripped on her breast,
  And her own in the shroud lay stark ;
And ' God forgive us, mother,' she said,
  ' We let it die in the dark ! '

EVARRA AND HIS GODS

Read here :
This is the story of Evarra—man—
Maker of Gods in lands beyond the sea.

Because the city gave him of her gold,

Because the caravans brought turquoises,

Because his life was sheltered by the King,

So that no man should maim him, none should
    steal,

Or break his rest with babble in the streets

When he was weary after toil, he made

An image of his God in gold and pearl,

With turquoise diadem and human eyes,

A wonder in the sunshine, known afar,

And worshipped by the King ; but, drunk with
    pride,

Because the city bowed to him for God,

He wrote above the shrine : ' *Thus Gods are made,*

' *And whoso makes them otherwise shall die.*'

And all the city praised him. . . . Then he died.

Read here the story of Evarra—man—
Maker of Gods in lands beyond the sea.

  Because the city had no wealth to give,
  Because the caravans were spoiled afar,
  Because his life was threatened by the King,
  So that all men despised him in the streets,
  He hewed the living rock, with sweat and tears,
  And reared a God against the morning-gold,
  A terror in the sunshine, seen afar,
  And worshipped by the King ; but, drunk with
      pride,
  Because the city fawned to bring him back,
  He carved upon the plinth : ' *Thus Gods are made,*
  ' *And whoso makes them otherwise shall die.*'
  And all the people praised him   . . Then he
      died.

Read here the story of Evarra—man—
Maker of Gods in lands beyond the sea.

  Because he lived among a simple folk,
  Because his village was between the hills,
  Because he smeared his cheeks with blood of ewes,
  He cut an idol from a fallen pine,
  Smeared blood upon its cheeks, and wedged a shell

Above its brows for eyes, and gave it hair
Of trailing moss, and plaited straw for crown.
And all the village praised him for this craft,
And brought him butter, honey, milk, and curds.
Wherefore, because the shoutings drove him mad,
He scratched upon that log : ' *Thus Gods are made,*
' *And whoso makes them otherwise shall die.*'
And all the people praised him. . . . Then he
    died.

Read here the story of Evarra—man—
Maker of Gods in lands beyond the sea.
    Because his God decreed one clot of blood
    Should swerve one hair's-breadth from the pulse's
        path,
    And chafe his brain, Evarra mowed alone,
    Rag-wrapped, among the cattle in the fields,
    Counting his fingers, jesting with the trees,
    And mocking at the mist, until his God
    Drove him to labour.   Out of dung and horns
    Dropped in the mire he made a monstrous God,
    Abhorrent, shapeless, crowned with plantain tufts,
    And when the cattle lowed at twilight-time,
    He dreamed it was the clamour of lost crowds,

And howled among the beasts : ' *Thus Gods are
    made,*
' *And whoso makes them otherwise shall die.*'
Thereat the cattle bellowed. . . . Then he died.

Yet at the last he came to Paradise,
And found his own four Gods, and that he wrote ;
And marvelled, being very near to God,
What oaf on earth had made his toil God's law,
Till God said mocking : ' Mock not. These be
    thine.'
Then cried Evarra : ' I have sinned ! '—' Not so.
' If thou hadst written otherwise, thy Gods
' Had rested in the mountain and the mine,
' And I were poorer by four wondrous Gods,
' And thy more wondrous law, Evarra.   Thine,
' Servant of shouting crowds and lowing kine.'

Thereat, with laughing mouth, but tear-wet eyes,
Evarra cast his Gods from Paradise.

This is the story of Evarra—man—
Maker of Gods in lands beyond the sea.

THE CONUNDRUM OF THE WORKSHOPS

When the flush of a new-born sun fell first on
    Eden's green and gold,
Our father Adam sat under the Tree and scratched
    with a stick in the mould ;
And the first rude sketch that the world had seen
    was joy to his mighty heart,
Till the Devil whispered behind the leaves, ' It's
    pretty, but is it Art ? '

Wherefore he called to his wife, and fled to fashion
    his work anew—
The first of his race who cared a fig for the first
    most dread review ;
And he left his lore to the use of his sons—and
    that was a glorious gain
When the Devil chuckled ' Is it Art ? ' in the ear
    of the branded Cain.

They builded a tower to shiver the sky and wrench
    the stars apart,
Till the Devil grunted behind the bricks : ' It 's
    striking, but is it Art ? '
The stone was dropped at the quarry-side and the
    idle derrick swung,
While each man talked of the aims of Art, and
    each in an alien tongue.

They fought and they talked in the North and
    the South, they talked and they fought in
    the West,
Till the waters rose on the pitiful land, and the
    poor Red Clay had rest—
Had rest till the dank blank-canvas dawn when the
    dove was preened to start,
And the Devil bubbled below the keel : ' It 's
    human, but is it Art ? '

The tale is as old as the Eden Tree—and new as
    the new-cut tooth—
For each man knows ere his lip-thatch grows he is
    master of Art and Truth ;

And each man hears as the twilight nears, to the
 beat of his dying heart,
The Devil drum on the darkened pane : ' You did
 it, but was it Art ? '

We have learned to whittle the Eden Tree to the
 shape of a surplice-peg,
We have learned to bottle our parents twain in the
 yelk of an addled egg,
We know that the tail must wag the dog, for the
 horse is drawn by the cart ;
But the Devil whoops, as he whooped of old : ' It 's
 clever, but is it Art ? '

When the flicker of London sun falls faint on the
 Club-room's green and gold,
The sons of Adam sit them down and scratch with
 their pens in the mould—
They scratch with their pens in the mould of their
 graves, and the ink and the anguish start,
For the Devil mutters behind the leaves :   It 's
 pretty, but is it Art ? '

Now, if we could win to the Eden Tree where the
    Four Great Rivers flow,
And the Wreath of Eve is red on the turf as she
    left it long ago,
And if we could come when the sentry slept and
    softly scurry through,
By the favour of God we might know as much—
    as our father Adam knew.

THE LEGEND OF EVIL

I

THIS is the sorrowful story
    Told when the twilight fails
And the monkeys walk together
    Holding each other's tails :—

' Our fathers lived in the forest,
    ' Foolish people were they,
' They went down to the cornland
    ' To teach the farmers to play.

' Our fathers frisked in the millet,
    ' Our fathers skipped in the wheat,
' Our fathers hung from the branches,
    ' Our fathers danced in the street.

' Then came the terrible farmers,
    ' Nothing of play they knew,
' Only . . . they caught our fathers
    ' And set them to labour too !

' Set them to work in the cornland
   ' With ploughs and sickles and flails,
' Put them in mud-walled prisons
   ' And—cut off their beautiful tails.

' Now, we can watch our fathers,
   ' Sullen and bowed and old,
' Stooping over the millet,
   ' Sharing the silly mould,

' Driving a foolish furrow,
   ' Mending a muddy yoke,
' Sleeping in mud-walled prisons,
   ' Steeping their food in smoke.

' We may not speak to our fathers
   ' For if the farmers knew
' They would come up to the forest
   ' And set us to labour too.'

This is the horrible story
   Told as the twilight fails
And the monkeys walk together
   Holding each other's tails.

II

'Twas when the rain fell steady an' the Ark was
    pitched an' ready,
  That Noah got his orders for to take the bastes
    below ;
He dragged them all together by the horn an' hide
    an' feather,
  An' all excipt the Donkey was agreeable to go

Thin Noah spoke him fairly, thin talked to him
    severely,
  An' thin he cursed him squarely to the glory av
    the Lord :—
' Divil take the ass that bred you, and the greater
    ass that fed you—
  ' Divil go wid you, ye spalpeen ! ' an' the Donkey
    went aboard.

But the wind was always failin', an' 'twas most
    onaisy sailin',
  An' the ladies in the cabin couldn't stand the
    stable air ;

An' the bastes betwuxt the hatches, they tuk an'
    died in batches,
  Till Noah said :—' There 's wan av us that hasn't
    paid his fare ! '

For he heard a flusteration wid the bastes av all
    creation—
  The trumpetin' av elephints an' bellowin' av
    whales ;
An' he saw forninst the windy whin he wint to
    stop the shindy
  The Divil wid a stable-fork bedivillin' their tails.

The Divil cursed outrageous, but Noah said um-
    brageous :—
  ' To what am I indebted for this tenant-right
    invasion ? '
An' the Divil gave for answer :—' Evict me if you
    can, sir,
  ' For I came in wid the Donkey—on Your
    Honour's invitation.'

THE ENGLISH FLAG

Above the portico a flag-staff, bearing the Union Jack, remained fluttering in the flames for some time, but ultimately when it fell the crowds rent the air with shouts, and seemed to see significance in the incident.

DAILY PAPERS.

WINDS of the World, give answer! They are
    whimpering to and fro—
And what should they know of England who only
    England know?—
The poor little street-bred people that vapour and
    fume and brag,
They are lifting their heads in the stillness to yelp
    at the English Flag!

Must we borrow a clout from the Boer—to plaster
    anew with dirt?
An Irish liar's bandage, or an English coward's
    shirt?
We may not speak of England: her Flag's to sell or
    share.
What is the Flag of England? Winds of the
    World, declare!

The North Wind blew :—' From Bergen my steel-
　　shod van-guards go ;
' I chase your lazy whalers home from the Disko floe ;
' By the great North Lights above me I work the
　　will of God,
' And the liner splits on the ice-field or the Dogger
　　fills with cod.

' I barred my gates with iron, I shuttered my doors
　　with flame,
' Because to force my ramparts your nutshell navies
　　came ;
' I took the sun from their presence, I cut them
　　down with my blast,
' And they died, but the Flag of England blew free
　　ere the spirit passed.

' The lean white bear hath seen it in the long, long
　　Arctic night,
' The musk-ox knows the standard that flouts the
　　Northern Light :
' What is the Flag of England ?　Ye have but my
　　bergs to dare,
' Ye have but my drifts to conquer.　Go forth, for it
　　is there ! '

The South Wind sighed :—' From the Virgins my
　　mid-sea course was ta'en
' Over a thousand islands lost in an idle main,
' Where the sea-egg flames on the coral and the
　　long-backed breakers croon
　Their endless ocean legends to the lazy, locked
　　lagoon.

' Strayed amid lonely islets, mazed amid outer
　　keys,
' I waked the palms to laughter—I tossed the scud in
　　the breeze—
' Never was isle so little, never was sea so lone,
' But over the scud and the palm-trees an English
　　flag was flown.

' I have wrenched it free from the halliard to hang
　　for a wisp on the Horn ;
' I have chased it north to the Lizard—ribboned and
　　rolled and torn ;
' I have spread its folds o'er the dying, adrift in a
　　hopeless sea ;
　I have hurled it swift on the slaver, and seen the
　　slave set free.

' My basking sunfish know it, and wheeling albatross,
' Where the lone wave fills with fire beneath the
    Southern Cross.
' What is the Flag of England ?   Ye have but my
    reefs to dare,
  Ye have but my seas to furrow.   Go forth, for it is
    there ! '

The East Wind roared :—' From the Kuriles, the
    Bitter Seas, I come,
' And me men call the Home-Wind, for I bring the
    English home.
' Look—look well to your shipping !   By the breath
    of my mad typhoon
' I swept your close-packed Praya and beached your
    best at Kowloon !

' The reeling junks behind me and the racing seas
    before,
' I raped your richest roadstead—I plundered Singa-
    pore !
' I set my hand on the Hoogli ; as a hooded snake
    she rose,
' And I flung your stoutest steamers to roost with
    the startled crows.

M

'Never the lotos closes, never the wild-fowl wake,

'But a soul goes out on the East Wind that died for
England's sake—

'Man or woman or suckling, mother or bride or
maid—

'Because on the bones of the English the English
Flag is stayed.

'The desert-dust hath dimmed it, the flying wild-ass
knows,

'The scared white leopard winds it across the taint-
less snows.

'What is the Flag of England ? Ye have but my
sun to dare,

'Ye have but my sands to travel.   Go forth, for it is
there ! '

The West Wind called :—' In squadrons the thought-
less galleons fly

'That bear the wheat and cattle lest street-bred
people die.

'They make my might their porter, they make my
house their path,

'Till I loose my neck from their rudder and whelm
them all in my wrath.

'I draw the gliding fog-bank as a snake is drawn
from the hole,
'They bellow one to the other, the frighted ship-
bells toll,
'For day is a drifting terror till I raise the shroud
with my breath,
'And they see strange bows above them and the
two go locked to death.

'But whether in calm or wrack-wreath, whether by
dark or day,
'I heave them whole to the conger or rip their
plates away,
'First of the scattered legions, under a shrieking sky,
'Dipping between the rollers, the English Flag goes
by.

'The dead dumb fog hath wrapped it—the frozen
dews have kissed—
'The naked stars have seen it, a fellow-star in the
mist.
'What is the Flag of England ? Ye have but my
breath to dare,
'Ye have but my waves to conquer. Go forth, for it
is there ! '

·CLEARED·

(IN MEMORY OF A COMMISSION)

HELP for a patriot distressed, a spotless spirit
hurt,
Help for an honourable clan sore trampled in the
dirt !
From Queenstown Bay to Donegal, O listen to my
song,
The honourable gentlemen have suffered grievous
wrong.

Their noble names were mentioned—O the burning
black disgrace !—
By a brutal Saxon paper in an Irish shooting-
case ;
They sat upon it for a year, then steeled their heart
to brave it,
And ' coruscating innocence ' the learned Judges
gave it.

Bear witness, Heaven, of that grim crime beneath
    the surgeon's knife,
The honourable gentlemen deplored the loss of
    life !
Bear witness of those chanting choirs that burk and
    shirk and snigger,
No man laid hand upon the knife or finger to the
    trigger !

Cleared in the face of all mankind beneath the
    winking skies,
Like phœnixes from Phœnix Park (and what lay
    there) they rise !
Go shout it to the emerald seas—give word to Erin
    now,
Her honourable gentlemen are cleared—and this
    is how :—

They only paid the Moonlighter his cattle-hocking
    price,
They only helped the murderer with counsel's best
    advice,

But—sure it keeps their honour white—the learned
    Court believes
They never give a piece of plate to murderers and
    thieves.

They never told the ramping crowd to card a
    woman's hide,
They never marked a man for death—what fault of
    theirs he died ?—
They only said ' intimidate,' and talked and went
    away—
By God, the boys that did the work were braver
    men than they !

Their sin it was that fed the fire—small blame to
    them that heard—
The ' bhoys ' get drunk on rhetoric, and madden
    at a word—
They knew whom they were talking at, if they
    were Irish too,
The gentlemen that lied in Court, they knew, and
    well they knew.

They only took the Judas-gold from Fenians out of
    jail,
They only fawned for dollars on the blood-dyed
    Clan-na-Gael.
If black is black or white is white, in black and
    white it 's down,
They 're only traitors to the Queen and rebels to
    the Crown.

' Cleared,' honourable gentlemen.   Be thankful it 's
    no more :——-
The widow's curse is on your house, the dead are
    at your door.
On you the shame of open shame, on you from
    North to South
The hand of every honest man flat-heeled across
    your mouth.

' Less black than we are painted ' ?—Faith, no
    word of black was said ;
The lightest touch was human blood, and that, you
    know, runs red.

It 's sticking to your fist to-day for all your sneer
    and scoff,
And by the Judge's well-weighed word you cannot
    wipe it off

Hold up those hands of innocence—go, scare your
    sheep together,
The blundering, tripping tups that bleat behind the
    old bell-wether ;
And if they snuff the taint and break to find
    another pen,
Tell them it 's tar that glistens so, and daub them
    yours again '

' The charge is old ' ?—As old as Cain—as fresh as
    yesterday ;
Old as the Ten Commandments—have ye talked
    those laws away ?
If words are words, or death is death, or powder
    sends the ball,
You spoke the words that sped the shot—the curse
    be on you all.

'Our friends believe'? Of course they do—-as
    sheltered women may ;
But have they seen the shrieking soul ripped from
    the quivering clay ?
They !—If their own front door is shut, they 'll
    swear the whole world 's warm ;
What do they know of dread of death or hanging
    fear of harm ?

The secret half a county keeps, the whisper in the
    lane,
The shriek that tells the shot went home behind
    the broken pane,
The dry blood crisping in the sun that scares the
    honest bees,
And shows the ' bhoys ' have heard your talk—what
    do they know of these ?

But you—you know—ay, ten times more ; the
    secrets of the dead,
Black terror on the country-side by word and
    whisper bred,

The mangled stallion's scream at night, the tail-
    cropped heifer's low.
Who set the whisper going first ?   You know, and
    well you know !

My soul ! I 'd sooner lie in jail for murder plain
    and straight,
Pure crime I 'd done with my own hand for money,
    lust, or hate,
Than take a seat in Parliament by fellow-felons
    cheered,
While one of those ' not provens ' proved me cleared
    as you are cleared.

Cleared—you that ' lost ' the League accounts—go,
    guard our honour still,
Go, help to make our country's laws that broke
    God's law at will—
One hand stuck out behind the back, to signal
    ' strike again ' ;
The other on your dress-shirt-front to show your
    heart is clane.

If black is black or white is white, in black and
    white it 's down,
You 're only traitors to the Queen and rebels to the
    Crown.
If print is print or words are words, the learned
    Court perpends :—
We are not ruled by murderers, but only—by their
    friends.

AN IMPERIAL RESCRIPT

Now this is the tale of the Council the German
 Kaiser decreed,
To ease the strong of their burden, to help the
 weak in their need,
He sent a word to the peoples, who struggle, and
 pant, and sweat,
That the straw might be counted fairly and the
 tally of bricks be set.

The Lords of Their Hands assembled ; from the
 East and the West they drew—
Baltimore, Lille, and Essen, Brummagem, Clyde,
 and Crewe.
And some were black from the furnace, and some
 were brown from the soil,
And some were blue from the dye-vat ; but all were
 wearied of toil.

And the young King said :—' I have found it, the
    road to the rest ye seek :

' The strong shall wait for the weary, the hale shall
    halt for the weak ;

' With the even tramp of an army where no man
    breaks from the line,

' Ye shall march to peace and plenty in the bond of
    brotherhood—sign ! '

The paper lay on the table, the strong heads bowed
    thereby.

And a wail went up from the peoples :—' Ay, sign—
    give rest, for we die ! '

A hand was stretched to the goose-quill, a fist was
    cramped to scrawl,

When—the laugh of a blue-eyed maiden ran clear
    through the council-hall.

And each one heard Her laughing as each one saw
    Her plain—

Saidie, Mimi, or Olga, Gretchen, or Mary Jane.

And the Spirit of Man that is in Him to the light
    of the vision woke ;

And the men drew back from the paper, as a
    Yankee delegate spoke :—

' There 's a girl in Jersey City who works on the
    telephone ;
' We 're going to hitch our horses and dig for a
    house of our own,
' With gas and water connections, and steam heat
    through to the top ;
' And, W. Hohenzollern, I guess I shall work till J
    drop.'

And an English delegate thundered :—' The weak
    an' the lame be blowed !
' I 've a berth in the Sou'-West workshops, a home
    in the Wandsworth Road ;
' And till the 'sociation has footed my buryin' bill,
' I work for the kids an' the missus. Pull up ! I 'll
    be damned if I will ! '

And over the German benches the bearded whisper
    ran :—
' Lager, der girls und der dollars, dey makes or dey
    breaks a man.
' If Schmitt haf collared der dollars, he collars der
    girl deremit ;
' But if Schmitt bust in der pizness, we collars der
    girl from Schmitt.'

They passed one resolution :—' Your sub-committee
believe

' You can lighten the curse of Adam when you 've
lightened the curse of Eve.

' But till we are built like angels, with hammer and
chisel and pen,

' We will work for ourself and a woman, for ever and
ever, amen.'

Now this is the tale of the Council the German
Kaiser held—

The day that they razored the Grindstone, the
day that the Cat was belled.

The day of the Figs from Thistles, the day of the
Twisted Sands,

The day that the laugh of a maiden made light of
the Lords of Their Hands.

TOMLINSON

Now Tomlinson gave up the ghost in his house in
    Berkeley Square,
And a Spirit came to his bedside and gripped him
    by the hair—
A Spirit gripped him by the hair and carried him
    far away,
Till he heard as the roar of a rain-fed ford the roar
    of the Milky Way :
Till he heard the roar of the Milky Way die down
    and drone and cease,
And they came to the Gate within the Wall where
    Peter holds the keys.
'Stand up, stand up now, Tomlinson, and answer
    loud and high
'The good that ye did for the sake of men or ever
    ye came to die—
'The good that ye did for the sake of men in little
    earth so lone ! '

And the naked soul of Tomlinson grew white as
    a rain-washed bone.

' O I have a friend on earth,' he said, ' that was
    my priest and guide,

' And well would he answer all for me if he were by
    my side.'

  ' For that ye strove in neighbour-love it shall be
    written fair,

' But now ye wait at Heaven's Gate and not in
    Berkeley Square :

' Though we called your friend from his bed this
    night, he could not speak for you,

' For the race is run by one and one and never by
    two and two.'

Then Tomlinson looked up and down, and little
    gain was there,

For the naked stars grinned overhead, and he saw
    that his soul was bare :

The Wind that blows between the worlds, it cut
    him like a knife,

And Tomlinson took up his tale and spoke of his
    good in life.

' This I have read in a book,' he said, ' and that was
    told to me,

N

' And this I have thought that another man thought
  of a Prince in Muscovy.'

The good souls flocked like homing doves and
  bade him clear the path,

And Peter twirled the jangling keys in weariness
  and wrath.

' Ye have read, ye have heard, ye have thought,' he
  said, ' and the tale is yet to run :

' By the worth of the body that once ye had, give
  answer—what ha' ye done ? '

Then Tomlinson looked back and forth, and little
  good it bore,

For the Darkness stayed at his shoulder-blade and
  Heaven's Gate before :—

' O this I have felt, and this I have guessed, and
  this I have heard men say,

' And this they wrote that another man wrote of a
  carl in Norroway.'

' Ye have read, ye have felt, ye have guessed, good
  lack !   Ye have hampered Heaven's Gate ;

' There 's little room between the stars in idleness to
  prate !

' O none may reach by hired speech of neighbour,
  priest, and kin

'Through borrowed deed to God's good meed that
lies so fair within ;

'Get hence, get hence to the Lord of Wrong, for
doom has yet to run,

'And . . . the faith that ye share with Berkeley
Square uphold you, Tomlinson ! '

.   .   .   .

The Spirit gripped him by the hair, and sun by sun
they fell

Till they came to the belt of Naughty Stars that
rim the mouth of Hell :

The first are red with pride and wrath, the next are
white with pain,

But the third are black with clinkered sin that
cannot burn again :

They may hold their path, they may leave their
path, with never a soul to mark,

They may burn or freeze, but they must not cease
in the Scorn of the Outer Dark.

The Wind that blows between the worlds, it nipped
him to the bone,

And he yearned to the flare of Hell-gate there as
the light of his own hearth-stone.

The Devil he sat behind the bars, where the desperate
legions drew,

But he caught the hasting Tomlinson and would not
let him through.

' Wot ye the price of good pit-coal that I must
pay ? ' said he,

' That ye rank yoursel' so fit for Hell and ask no
leave of me ?

' I am all o'er-sib to Adam's breed that ye should
give me scorn,

' For I strove with God for your First Father the day
that he was born.

' Sit down, sit down upon the slag, and answer loud
and high

' The harm that ye did to the Sons of Men or ever
you came to die.'

And Tomlinson looked up and up, and saw against
the night

The belly of a tortured star blood-red in Hell-
Mouth light ;

And Tomlinson looked down and down, and saw
beneath his feet

The frontlet of a tortured star milk-white in Hell-
Mouth heat.

' O I had a love on earth,' said he, ' that kissed
    me to my fall,

' And if ye would call my love to me I know she
    would answer all.'

—' All that ye did in love forbid it shall be written
    fair,

' But now ye wait at Hell-Mouth Gate and not in
    Berkeley Square :

' Though we whistled your love from her bed to-night,
    I trow she would not run,

' For the sin ye do by two and two ye must pay for
    one by one ! '

The Wind that blows between the worlds, it cut him
    like a knife,

And Tomlinson took up the tale and spoke of his
    sin in life :—

' Once I ha' laughed at the power of Love and twice
    at the grip of the Grave,

' And thrice I ha' patted my God on the head that
    men might call me brave.'

The Devil he blew on a brandered soul and set it
    aside to cool :—

' Do ye think I would waste my good pit-coal on the
    hide of a brain-sick fool ?

' I see no worth in the hobnailed mirth or the jolt-
head jest ye did

' That I should waken my gentlemen that are sleeping three on a grid.'

Then Tomlinson looked back and forth, and there
was little grace,

For Hell-Gate filled the houseless Soul with the
Fear of Naked Space.

' Nay, this I ha' heard,' quo' Tomlinson, ' and this
was noised abroad,

' And this I ha' got from a Belgian book on the word
of a dead French lord.'

—' Ye ha' heard, ye ha' read, ye ha' got, good lack !
and the tale begins afresh—

' Have ye sinned one sin for the pride o' the eye or
the sinful lust of the flesh ? '

Then Tomlinson he gripped the bars and yammered,
' Let me in—

' For I mind that I borrowed my neighbour's wife to
sin the deadly sin.'

The Devil he grinned behind the bars, and banked
the fires high :

' Did ye read of that sin in a book ? ' said he ; and
Tomlinson said, ' Ay ! '

The Devil he blew upon his nails, and the little
    devils ran,

And he said, ' Go husk this whimpering thief that
    comes in the guise of a man :

' Winnow him out 'twixt star and star, and sieve his
    proper worth :

' There 's sore decline in Adam's line if this be spawn
    of earth.'

Empusa's crew, so naked-new they may not face the
    fire,

But weep that they bin too small to sin to the height
    of their desire,

Over the coal they chased the Soul, and racked it
    all abroad,

As children rifle a caddis-case or the raven's foolish
    hoard.

And back they came with the tattered Thing, as
    children after play,

And they said : ' The soul that he got from God he
    has bartered clean away.

' We have threshed a stook of print and book, and
    winnowed a chattering wind,

' And many a soul wherefrom he stole, but his we
    cannot find :

' We have handled him, we have dandled him, we
    have seared him to the bone,

' And sure if tooth and nail show truth he has no soul
    of his own.'

The Devil he bowed his head on his breast and
    rumbled deep and low :—

'I 'm all o'er-sib to Adam's breed that I should bid
    him go.

' Yet close we lie, and deep we lie, and if I gave him
    place,

' My gentlemen that are so proud would flout me to
    my face ;

' They 'd call my house a common stews and me a
    careless host,

' And—I would not anger my gentlemen for the sake
    of a shiftless ghost.'

The Devil he looked at the mangled Soul that
    prayed to feel the flame,

And he thought of Holy Charity, but he thought of
    his own good name :—

' Now ye could haste my coal to waste, and sit ye
    down to fry :

' Did ye think of that theft for yourself ? ' said he :
    and Tomlinson said, ' Ay ! '

The Devil he blew an outward breath, for his heart
    was free from care :—

' Ye have scarce the soul of a louse,' he said, ' but
    the roots of sin are there,

' And for that sin should ye come in were I the lord
    alone.

' But sinful pride has rule inside—and mightier than
    my own.

' Honour and Wit, fore-damned they sit, to each his
    priest and whore :

' Nay, scarce I dare myself go there, and you they 'd
    torture sore.

' Ye are neither spirit nor spirk,' he said ; ' ye are
    neither book nor brute—

' Go, get ye back to the flesh again for the sake of
    Man's repute.

' I 'm all o'er-sib to Adam's breed that I should mock
    your pain,

' But look that ye win to worthier sin ere ye come
    back again.

' Get hence, the hearse is at your door—the grim
    black stallions wait—

' They bear your clay to place to-day. Speed, lest
    ye come too late !

' Go back to Earth with a lip unsealed—go back
    with an open eye,
' And carry my word to the Sons of Men or ever ye
    come to die :
' That the sin they do by two and two they must pay
    for one by one—
' And . . . the God that you took from a printed
    book be with you, Tomlinson ' '

L'ENVOI

THERE's a whisper down the field where the year
      has shot her yield,
  And the ricks stand grey to the sun,
Singing :—' Over then, come over, for the bee has
      quit the clover,
' And your English summer 's done.'
          You have heard the beat of the offshore wind,
          And the thresh of the deep-sea rain ;
          You have heard the song—how long ! how
              long ?
          Pull out on the trail again.

          Ha' done with the Tents of Shem, dear lass,
          We 've seen the seasons through,
          And it 's time to turn on the old trail, our own
              trail, the out trail,
          Pull out, pull out, on the Long Trail—the trail
              that is always new.

203

It 's North you may run to the rime-ringed sun,
　Or South to the blind Horn's hate ;
Or East all the way into Mississippi Bay,
　Or West to the Golden Gate :
　　Where the blindest bluffs hold good, dear
　　　lass,
　　And the wildest tales are true,
　　And the men bulk big on the old trail, our own
　　　trail, the out trail,
　　And life runs large on the Long Trail—the
　　　trail that is always new.

The days are sick and cold, and the skies are grey
　　and old,
　And the twice-breathed airs blow damp ;
And I 'd sell my tired soul for the bucking beam-sea
　　roll
　Of a black Bilbao tramp ;
　　With her load-line over her hatch, dear lass,
　　And a drunken Dago crew,
　　And her nose held down on the old trail, our
　　　own trail, the out trail,
　　From Cadiz Bar on the Long Trail—the trail
　　　that is always new.

There be triple ways to take, of the eagle or the
    snake,
  Or the way of a man with a maid ;
But the sweetest way to me is a ship's upon the sea
  In the heel of the North-East Trade.
    Can you hear the crash on her bows, dear lass,
    And the drum of the racing screw,
    As she ships it green on the old trail, our own
      trail, the out trail,
    As she lifts and 'scends on the Long Trail—
      the trail that is always new ?

See the shaking funnels roar, with the Peter at the
    fore,
  And the fenders grind and heave,
And the derricks clack and grate, as the tackle
    hooks the crate,
  And the fall-rope whines through the sheave ;
    It's ' Gang-plank up and in,' dear lass,
    It's ' Hawsers warp her through ! '
    And it's ' All clear aft ' on the old trail, our
      own trail, the out trail,
    We're backing down on the Long Trail—the
      trail that is always new.

O the mutter overside, when the port-fog holds us tied,
    And the sirens hoot their dread !
When foot by foot we creep o'er the hueless viewless
      deep
    To the sob of the questing lead !
      It's down by the Lower Hope, dear lass,
      With the Gunfleet Sands in view,
      Till the Mouse swings green on the old trail,
        our own trail, the out trail,
      And the Gull Light lifts on the Long Trail—
        the trail that is always new.

O the blazing tropic night, when the wake's a
      welt of light
    That holds the hot sky tame,
And the steady fore-foot snores through the planet
      powdered floors
    Where the scared whale flukes in flame !
      Her plates are scarred by the sun, dear lass,
      And her ropes are taunt with the dew,
      For we're booming down on the old trail, our
        own trail, the out trail,
      We're sagging south on the Long Trail—the
        trail that is always new.

Then home, get her home, where the drunken
      rollers comb,
  And the shouting seas drive by,
And the engines stamp and ring, and the wet bows
      reel and swing,
  And the Southern Cross rides high !
    Yes, the old lost stars wheel back, dear lass,
    That blaze in the velvet blue.
    They 're all old friends on the old trail, our
      own trail, the out trail,
    They 're God's own guides on the Long Trail—
      the trail that is always new.

Fly forward, O my heart, from the Foreland to the
      Start—
  We 're steaming all-too slow,
And it 's twenty thousand mile to our little lazy isle
  Where the trumpet-orchids blow !
    You have heard the call of the off-shore wind
    And the voice of the deep-sea rain ;
    You have heard the song—how long ! how
      long ?
    Pull out on the trail again !

The Lord knows what we may find, dear lass,
And The Deuce knows what we may do—
But we're back once more on the old trail, our
    own trail, the out trail,
We're down, hull down on the Long Trail—
    the trail that is always new.